Journey to Success

Developing a Personal Success Strategic Plan (PSSP)

Program Facilitator's Guide

Copyright 2013 Moovin4ward Presentations LLC

Library of Congress Control Number: 2013919720

ISBN: Paperback 978-0-9884564-95

All rights reserved. No part of this book may be reproduced or transmitted in any form or by any means, electronic or mechanical, including photocopying, recording, or by any information storage and retrieval systems, without permission in writing from the publisher.

Published by   Moovin4ward Publishing
P.O. Box 22436
Huntsville, AL 35814

Printed in the United States of America.

To order copies of the accompanying workbook at bulk pricing, contact,

    Moovin4ward Presentations
    1-888-893-6303
    orders@moovin4ward.com
    www.journey2successPSSP.com

Look for the book, *Mapping Your Journey to Success: Six Steps to Personal Planning*, to accompany this program. You can find it at the www.journey2successPSSP.com website or Amazon.com.

To become a Certified PSSP Facilitator, email **pssp@moovin4ward.com** or visit **www.journey2successPSSP.com/affiliation_program.htm**.

Contents

Getting Started 7
- How to Use this Guide 7
- Facilitating the Program 8
- Managing the Program 9
- Evaluating the Workshop 11

Facilitating the Key Concepts 13

Program Agendas 19
- "Plenary" Session – One-Hour 19
- "Workshop" Session – Half-Day 19

Session 1: Destination & Purpose 21
- A Journey to Barcelona 23
- Six Steps to PSSP 25
- DNA of Successful People 27
- True Meaning of Success 28
- It All Starts with You 30
- Purpose Statement 35

Session 2: Goals & Strategies 37
- Set SMART Goals 41
- Personal SWOT Analysis 45
- Developing Strategies 50

Session 3: Action & Progress 53
- Positive Attitude 55
- Law of Attraction 56
- Hard Work 64
- Self-Motivation 65
- Progress Evaluation Process 71

Session 4: PSSP Review & Challenge 77
- Action Plan Format 79
- The PSSP Challenge 81

Plenary Session Script 83

PSSP Template 111

Getting Started

The Journey to Success (J2S) program was developed to help individuals to develop a Personal Success Strategic Plan (PSSP) using the outlined six steps. The program is based on the book, *Mapping Your Journey to Success: Six Steps to Personal Planning*, written by Sharon A. Myers and Mark Wiggins.

Whether you're an experienced facilitator or a novice instructor, you'll find that this guide is a useful resource for facilitating and managing the J2S program. This guide provides you with the script of the sessions to include instructions for facilitating the discussions, exercises and activities. Screenshots of the participant's workbook pages are also included with the script so that you see what they see as you present the materials.

Before you get to the script, this guide provides you with a few techniques on how to effectively facilitate, manage, and evaluate the J2S program. You can create your own program presentation materials or purchase the "Program-In-A-Box" from Moovin4ward Presentations, which includes everything you need to get started immediately.

The J2S "Program-In-A-Box" includes:
1. A Participant Workbook (for the half-day format)
2. A Participant Worksheet (for the one-hour format)
3. Presentation & Challenge Slides
4. Presentation Activity Materials
5. Evaluation Forms

How to Use this Guide

Here are some suggestions for using this book effectively:

- **Be sure you understand the key concepts.** Spend some time studying this Guide along with the participant workbook to review the key concepts. Also consider reading the book, *Mapping Your Journey to Success, Six Steps to Personal Planning*.

- **Review the entire program agenda.** Go through the entire agenda and script, adding notes as you go to ensure you understand the transitions and how to smoothly flow from one concept to the next.

- **Be sure you understand the activities and exercises.** This guide includes a variety of interactive activities and exercises. Use the activities and exercises to engage and challenge the attendees on the concepts to ensure that learning takes place.

- **Add your personal experience.** When facilitating the program, it enhances the content when you can provide real examples from your experiences. Also consider identifying successful leaders that you can reference as examples to ensure appropriateness for each audience.

Facilitating the Program

The term *facilitation* signifies the point at which we go beyond the concept of lecturing into interactive and experiential learning. We all know that learners remember 10 percent of what they hear; 20 percent of what they see; 65 percent of what they hear and see; and 90% of what they hear, see, and do.

This is the principle that drives the activities in this **Journey to Success** program. Your participants will be "doing" a lot in the sessions to ensure maximum retention of the skills they learn and practice here.

Workshop Preparations

1. It's best if you can set up your room the day before the session begins. This enables you to deal with any problems caused by missing or faulty equipment and ensures that you're not sweaty and worn out from moving tables and equipment when your attendees arrive.

2. Set up your facilitator table with your Guide and program materials. Load your CD player with suitable music, and turn on your computer with the Microsoft PowerPoint presentation loaded directly onto the hard drive. Be sure to bring a backup copy on a removable drive.

3. If there's a phone in the room, check to see what you have to do to silence it for the duration of the workshop. Find out how to operate the thermostat. Learn where the light switches are. And ask about fire exits and restroom locations if you are in a building where you don't normally work.

4. Be sure the room is set for the appropriate number of attendees. Take a seat in the back row as well as around the outer edges of the tables, to confirm that everyone will have a good view of the screen and of all activity at the front of the room.

5. When you feel confident that you've addressed all the details of your meeting room, prepare the site for your attendees.

Program Materials
Have the following items available when facilitating this program:

- Laptop with presentations slides and easy listening music
- Presentation Materials:
    donkey poster, donkey tails, map, plan, blindfold, agree/disagree cards and affirmation cards
- Projector & Screen
- Presentation on removable drive
- Facilitator's Program Script
- Two bottles of water
- Mints
- Headache remedies
- Stopwatch *(Smartphone timer... "There's an app for that!")*

Managing the Program

This section describes general techniques useful in maintaining control of your program.

Build Rapport

- ☑ **Extend a warm welcome.**
  Welcome participants with a warm smile and a handshake.

- ☑ **Call people by name.**
  Learn and use participants' first names.

- ☑ **Show interest.**
  Express interest in each individual. Find out what your participants want to learn.

- ☑ **Relax and have fun.**
  Show your sense of humor.

- ☑ **Be approachable.**
  Be accepting of participant comments and available to participants at breaks and lunch.

- ☑ **Look and listen.**
  Watch for participants' nonverbal messages such as puzzled looks or signs of discomfort. Listen to their comments and acknowledge their contributions.

Establish Credibility

- ☑ **Look professional.**
  Wear clean, pressed clothing that reflects the dress standards of the organization, the group you are training, the training site, and your gender. Pay attention to your hair, nails, and makeup. Good grooming creates a neat appearance that helps establish professional credibility.

- ☑ **Know your subject.**
  Study the key concepts, program script, and the directions for facilitating the learning activities and the assessments.

- ☑ **Speak clearly, distinctly, smoothly, and with authority.**
  Avoid slang, jargon, profanity, or other language that might offend. Verbal qualifiers such as "kind of" or "sort of" detract from your credibility. "Ums" and "ahs" convey the impression that you are unsure of or unfamiliar with your material.

- ☑ **Maintain good posture.**
  Communicate self-confidence and high self-esteem nonverbally by maintaining good posture.

☑ **Maintain eye contact.**
Look participants in the eye when you address them, as well as when you listen to their comments.

☑ **Use gestures for emphasis.**
Gestures can underscore key points, and make stories come alive.

Leading Discussions

☑ **Encourage idea exchange.**
Encourage participants to share ideas, experiences, supervision techniques, and systems knowledge, as well as to exchange opinions.

☑ **Involve everyone.**
Draw out shy or quiet individuals by giving them assignments; for instance, ask them to serve as recorder of the small group discussions.

☑ **Stay focused on the topic.**
Keep discussion focused on the topic. If a comment if off the subject, redirect it. You can also offer to discuss the matter during a break. If the point is on the topic that you will cover later, defer it.

☑ **Keep discussion positive.**
Keep discussions positive and constructive.

Bring a prize bag!
A prize bag is an optional item that's always a hit. Just load it up with rewards from your local dollar store or purchased from our PSSP catalog, which can be a fun incentive to get attendees into the spirit of competition.

Evaluating the Workshop

Evaluations, a valuable tool for improving your skills, are often overlooked. In many cases, evaluations are distributed in the last minutes of a session when participants are anxious to leave and unwilling to spend time giving meaningful comments.

In the same way that a current customer is our best tool for enhancing company performance, a participant who has just completed your program is the best barometer of the program's effectiveness, as well as your ability to facilitate learning.

Additionally, a presenter's willingness to be evaluated by the attendees sends an important message. If that facilitator is committed to continual improvement, it reminds the participants that they too, need to be willing to continue developing their abilities.

Evaluation Techniques

- Evaluation through class discussion can be useful if prefaced correctly. It's important to let the participants know that their comments are being accepted in the spirit of development and that you will not be offended by anything they say.

- Informal evaluations or interviews are also useful information-gathering tools. Simply visiting with those who have completed the program can give you ideas about which material worked and what revisions need to be made for the next presentation.

- Send a 30-day follow-up letter to the program coordinator asking if participants are using the information and techniques that were practiced in the workshop. This offers you an opportunity to receive additional evaluations of the program.

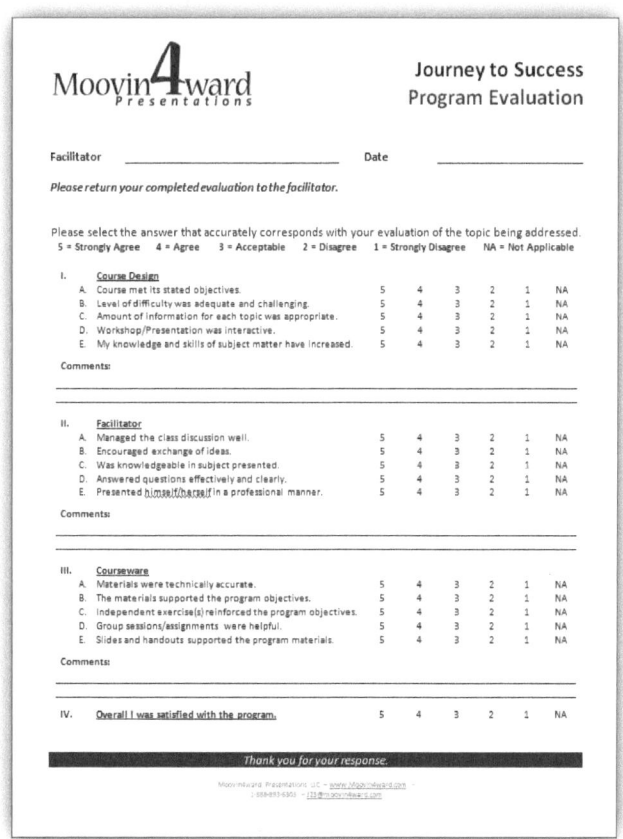

Personal Success Strategic Plan (PSSP)

Facilitating the Key Concepts

The goal of the Journey to Success program is to empower individuals to strategize for the future they wish to have. The program teaches participants some simple life changing techniques that help them to personalize their journey to success by developing a personal success strategic plan.

Objectives

This program provides participants with the Six Steps to Develop a Personal Success Strategic Plan. Upon completion of the program, participants will

- Understand where they want to go in life and why;
- Create better goals and strategies to achieve them;
- Use a positive attitude, self motivation, and hard work to keep moving forward; and
- Make adjustments when things don't go as planned.

1. Determine your Destination

Key Concept

Success is not one major event, but a series of achieved goals, that motivates you to continue to move toward your destination. This discussion will begin with identifying successful people and the common traits of those people. The intent of this discussion is to get the participants to think about their end destination… their personal success, however they define it. The participants will participate in a fun, interactive activity that helps them visualize what's needed to reach their destination.

Facilitation Tips

- Think of all the possible "tasks" that must be accomplished to make the trip to Barcelona happen.
- Ask the participants for additional tasks to involve them in the story.
- Tie the story back to planning for success.
- Enumerate the PSSP steps has your run through the overview.
- Allow time for participants to fill-in the names of successful people.
- Remind participants that they don't have to personally know the people they choose to list.
- Consider having participants read the "High Achievers" description.
- Acknowledge that their personal definition may be very different or very similar to society's definition… and that's okay!
- Summarize the "Determine Your Destination" step before moving to the next one.
- Be diverse in your selections of participants to bring forward for the Donkey activity.
- Debrief the Donkey activity in the correct order to emphasis the need for a plan last.
- Reference the Donkey activity, when appropriate, throughout the workshop.

2. Identify your Purpose

Key Concept
You can significantly increase the odds of success in any endeavor if you know who you are, what you want, where you're going, how you'll get there, and what you will do when you arrive. In this discussion, you will highlight specific elements that help define the participant's purpose.

You will provide participants with an in-depth discussion and examples on how to answer specific questions about themselves and their purpose for living. The participants are encouraged to use the answers to develop their personal purpose statement.

Facilitation Tips
- Inform participants that this journey begins with them.
- Provide the definition of each attribute FIRST. Then provide the "question" that the attribute answers.
- Allow participants time to write down their answers.
- Consider asking the participants for examples as you discuss each of the attributes.
- It is not required that all of the examples in the book be covered. Consider adding a few of your own.
- When completing the "Core Values" exercise, be sure to continue to repeat the instructions.
- Encourage participants to "truly" make the selections during the exercises.
- Re-emphasize how the purpose statement allows the participants to reach their "success" when reviewing the purpose statement activity.
- Reinforce that this is just the starting point; participants are only asked to "draft" a purpose statement which can be revisited later.
- Summarize the key concepts of "Identifying Purpose" and remind participants of the previous steps covered thus far.

3. Set SMART Goals

Key Concept
Setting goals makes life more meaningful and increases your level of optimism, ultimately leading to greater fulfillment and more achievement. In this discussion you will review the types and categories of goals, the importance of setting goals and the system for judging the attributes of goals.

To ensure that the participants understand the system, we will use case studies to analyze how the SMART system works. Participants will then have an opportunity to describe a few of their own goals within various categories.

Facilitation Tips

- Select a category on the worksheet to review with the group as an example before grouping the participants for the activity.
- Select a goal of yours that you can share OR ask a participant for a goal that you can use as an example to describe the SMART framework.
- Choose a goal that is relative to your audience (i.e. if college participants use college-related examples or if corporate participants, use work-related examples.)
- When completing the "Goal Setting Worksheet" it is not necessary to do each category.
- Be sure not to criticize anyone's goal, but consider asking how the SMART framework applies.
- Be sure to summarize the current step and remind participants of the previous steps covered thus far.

4. Develop your Strategy

Key Concept

Your strategy is your plan of action which you execute to accomplish your goals. What will you do to make success a reality based on the goals you've set and where you want to go to fulfill your purpose. It is easier to achieve your goals when your strategy maximizes your strengths, without exposing your weaknesses, while taking advantage of opportunities and mitigating personal threats. Participants will walk through the process of completing a personal SWOT analysis and developing strategies to achieve goals.

Facilitation Tips

- Have more than one "game" of strategy in mind (i.e. chess, checkers, tic-tac-toe).
- Reference your Journey to Barcelona strategy examples (i.e. learning Spanish).
- Use the review of the SWOT as a brainstorming session where participants may share out loud. This will help later when they are tasked to complete their own PSA.
- Answer whether a characteristic is a strength or a weaknesses, for example "perfectionism".
- Emphasize the need to be honest with the PSA, particularly with weaknesses and threats.
- Keep participation high, look for places to engage.
- Summarize the key concept of "Developing Your Strategies" and remind participants of the previous steps covered thus far.

5. Take Action

Key Concept

The best kept secret of success is that succes is always preceded by hard work, along with a positive attitude and self-motivation. In this portion of the program, we will highlight how the law of attraction affects our positive attitude; provide tips for self motivation, and review some well known successful people who simply used "hard word" to reach their destination. Participants will also learn how to craft and use visualization and affirmation techniques to help develop strategies.

Facilitation Tips

- Have a contest to see who can complete the grey box first and give an award to the winner. Be sure to have them read their answer aloud.
- Use LOTS of details to engage all of the senses for the participants when you share the visualization story.
- Use personal testimonials to demonstrate how positive affirmations have impacted your life.
- Allow adequate time for participants to write out the steps to crafting their affirmations.
- Provide recommendations on where to keep the card after the affirmation exercise.
- Remind groups participating in the "Visualization & Affirmation" exercise that they don't have to do all of the categories, just select three.
- Have some of your own examples of hardworking individuals to discuss.
- Tie the "hard work" emphasis back to the characteristics of the successful people listed in the first session.
- Engage participants in discussion on external and internal motivators. Encourage participants to use what works best for them.
- Call on participants to read the Self Motivation Tips before discussing.
- Summarize the concepts of "Taking Action" and remind participants of the previous steps covered thus far.

6. Evaluate your Progress

Key Concept

Your plan is not complete unless it includes opportunities to evaluate your progress along your journey. Participants will be encouraged to incorporate "checkpoints" into their journey towards success to evaluate their progress. Several participants will participate in an interactive exercise that uncovers some of the many myths on how to measure success. Using the Progress Evaluation Process (PEP), participants will be encouraged to reward themselves for successful accomplishment of small goals and to make adjustments to goals and strategies when detours are encountered.

Facilitation Tips

- Start by asking "how do you measure success?" and allow time for a few answers, but no discussion.
- Bring up a diverse group of individuals to participate in the Agree/Disagree exercise.
- Remind participants that there are no wrong or right answers.
- Keep the audience involved as you go through the questions (i.e. "how many of you agree or disagree?).
- Protect the participant when their answer differs greatly from the audience.
- Summarize the activity to ensure participants understand that "success is personal" and therefore cannot be measured and/or compared.

- Take your time stepping thru the flow chart. Consider asking a participant to step thru it for you.
- Emphasize the need to document accomplishments and reward successes.
- Have 1-3 participants read the second paragraph of "Documentation".
- Summarize all Six Steps. Consider having the participants call them out one at a time.

The PSSP Challenge

Participants will be engaged in a "game show" activity to help assess the participants' comprehension of the PSSP concepts in a fun and interactive way.

Facilitation Tips

- Check your system before the presentation to ensure you are free of technical difficulties.
- Go out strong after the challenge and be sure to tie all the activities together.
- Set up the room prior to asking for volunteers.
- Select your volunteers in advance or use the coordinator staff.
- Get at least two teams or more (up to 6) to participate, if time allows.
- Summarize all Six Steps.

Personal Success Strategic Plan (PSSP)

Program Agendas

"Workshop" Session – Half-Day

The full half-day program is broken into four sessions. Each of the first three sessions presents two of the Six PSSP Steps, while the final session presents a review of all topics and completion of a draft PSSP.

Agenda	Type	Duration	Session
SESSION ONE	**Destination & Purpose**		
Journey to Barcelona	Story	2	
PSSP Overview	Lecture	3	
Donkey Tail	Activity 1.1	10	
DNA of Successful People	Discussion	5	
True Meaning of Success	Discussion	5	
It Starts With You	Exercise	15	
Core Values	Activity 2.1	5	
Purpose for Living	Discussion	5	50
SESSION TWO	**Goals & Strategy**		
Importance of Goals	Lecture	2	
Goal Setting Worksheet	Activity 3.1	10	
SMART Goals	Exercise	10	
Personal SWOT Analysis	Discussion	5	
Completing Your PSA	Activity 4.1	10	
Developing Strategies	Exercise	3	
Plan of Action	Activity 4.2	10	50
SESSION THREE	**Action & Progress**		
Positive Attitude	Lecture	2	
Understanding Affirmations	Discussion	5	
Affirmation Cards	Activity 5.1	5	
Visualization & Affirmation	Activity 5.2	5	
Hard Work	Stories	3	
Self-Motivation	Discussion	5	
Measuring Success	Activity 6.1	10	
Progress Evaluation Process	Discussion	5	
Rewards & Documentation	Discussion	5	
Barriers to Success	Lecture	5	50
SESSION FOUR	**PSSP Review & Challenge**		
PSSP Template Review	Exercise	20	
PSSP Pyramid Game	Activity 7.1	30	50

"Plenary" Session – One-Hour

The one-hour program allows you to interactively hit all of the highlights in a shorter time frame, typically between 60-90 minutes.

Agenda	Type	Duration	Session
Description			
Journey to Barcelona	Story	2	
PSSP Overview	Lecture	1	
Donkey Tail	Activity	10	
True Meaning of Success	Discussion	3	
It Starts With You	Exercise	6	
Set SMART Goals	Lecture	5	
Plan of Action - Strategies	Discussion	5	
Positive Attitude	Lecture	1	
Affirmation	Exercise	2	
Hard Work	Stories	2	
Self-Motivation	Lecture	2	
Measuring Success	Activity	10	
Progress Evaluation Process	Discussion	4	
Barriers to Success	Exercise	5	
PSSP Review	Q&A	2	60

When more time is available (i.e. more than 60 minutes), use the time during the activities.

Workshop Script
Session 1: Destination & Purpose

A Journey to Barcelona

[2 minutes]

Let's go on a journey.

What is a journey? *[Wait for a few answers.]*

One definition states that a journey is an occasion when you travel from one place to another, especially when there is a long distance between the places.

Based on this definition, you need to know where YOU ARE and then the place YOU WANT TO GO.

So let's say we want to go to Barcelona, Spain. Every summer they host a huge carnival with an abundance of feasting, dancing, and partying in the streets. I've always dreamed of going there during that time. You would expect that this would be a journey of a lifetime, something you'll never forget. So you'll want to do more than a weekend visit.

So first, we'll go on the Internet to see how far away it is. Wow. That's a true journey. Is this really where we want to go? Yes! We only live once!

So what do we need to do to make this happen? *[Poll the participants for a list of things that may need to be done to make the journey happen. Expect responses such as: get a passport, find lodging, book a flight, learn the weather, buy new clothes, learn Spanish, etc.]*

It won't happen overnight. We'll need to make lots of arrangements and save some money. The goal is to get there within the next five years. We'll need a minimum of $10,000 in cash, because we don't want to do it on credit. We want to come home from our journey debt free and smiling.

So we will need to pay off all of our current debt then start to save the money for the trip. We'll need to get a passport. We'll need to find a place to stay that won't require us to need transportation right away, except for the taxi from the airport. We'll need to find out what the weather is like, so we'll know how to pack. We'll need to learn some Spanish, because we want to be able to communicate.

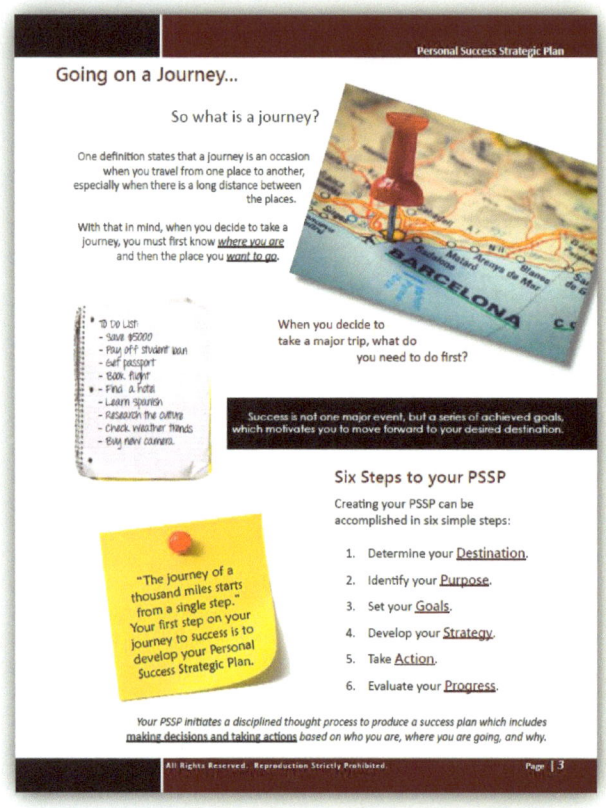

There's a lot to do. To make sure we stay on track, we may create a timeline with deadlines of when we want to complete our small goals, so that we can make it to Barcelona in the timeframe that we've scheduled.

Once we get our plan together, we can get started: saving money, learning Spanish, looking for housing, making our dream come true.

Now along the way, things may come up. I might lose my job, I might lose a loved one, I might encounter a medical emergency or natural disaster that depletes my savings... things, obstacles, unexpected challenges, might come along.

But when you are committed, it means that no matter what happens, you are going to fulfill your goal. Why? Because we have planned for it and want it badly, that's why. We may have to shift our schedule, stay at a lesser expensive hotel, or make other adjustments to the plan; but we are going to follow through with it.

In many ways, planning a big trip is like planning for success. You'll need to know where you're going, why you're going, and then develop goals and strategies to get there. You'll also need to expect the unexpected and monitor your progress along the way.

 **Success is not one major event, but a series of achieved goals, that motivates you to keep moving forward.**

It all starts with creating your own **Personal Success Strategic Plan (PSSP)** and taking action according to your plan to reach **your** defined success.

Developing a PSSP will help you to initiate a disciplined thought process to produce a success plan which includes _making decisions and taking_ action based on who you are, where you are going, and why.

Follow along with me on page 3 as I share the Six Steps to developing your PSSP.

Six Steps to PSSP

[3 minutes]

1. Determine Your **Destination**. It doesn't matter where you come from; the most important key is to determine where you want to go.

2. Identify Your **Purpose**. It is your compass that guides you and drives you to what you want to do with your life.

3. Set Your **Goals.** You need to have personal goals in life to which you can strive and which will make it easier to reach your destination.

4. Develop Your **Strategy.** Your strategies are the steps you plan to take in order to make your goals a reality.

5. Take **Action.** This is where you make it all happen; do what you've planned.

6. Evaluate Your **Progress**. Check yourself periodically to ensure you stay on track and make adjustments as needed.

Keep in mind that *"The journey of a thousand miles starts from a single step." Your first step on your journey to success starts with your Personal Success Strategic Plan.* Through the program, I will guide you to develop your own PSSP.

Journey to Success Program

Step #1: Determine Your Destination

Let's play a game. I'll need three volunteers to assist me. *[Select three diverse volunteers.]*

> **Activity 1.1: Donkey Tail**
>
> **Time:** 15 minutes
>
> **Materials:** Donkey poster, three donkey tails in a box hidden in the audience, 1 blindfold, 1 map, and 1 plan (list of specific instructions to find the hidden donkey tails).
>
> **Process:**
>
> We're going to play an old game, "Pin the Tail on the Donkey?" We're going to see which of your peers can pin the tail on the donkey first. *[Point to the donkey poster on the easel.]*
>
> Now, what is your name? Okay, Name 1, you get to be blindfolded. *[Tie blindfold on the first volunteer.]* What's your name? Okay, Name 2, you get this. *[Hand the second volunteer the map.]* And now what's your name? Okay, Name 3, you get this *[Hand student the instructions.]*
>
> Okay, you guys have 5 minutes to pin the tail on the donkey. Go! *[Don't give any additional instructions. Just let it play out. Once the third volunteer has pinned the tail on the donkey, call "TIME."]*
>
> So how was that? Let's start with Name1. Why didn't you pin the tail on the donkey? *[Allow discussion with the volunteer and the audience. We are looking for "couldn't see the donkey and/or it moved."]*
>
> How about you, Name 2. Why didn't you pin the tail on the donkey? You could see it and you had a map. *[Allow for discussion with the volunteer and the audience (i.e. "the map didn't help" or "it didn't give any information".]*
>
> And lastly, Name 3. Why was it so easy for you to pin the tail on the donkey? *[We are looking for "I could see where I needed to go," or "I had instructions."* So you had a plan that was specific to your goal?
>
> How helpful would it be to have a step-by-step plan for a successful life?

To be successful in life, it's important to define what success means to you personally. Your destination is your success. Once you've determined your destination, you can create step-by-step instructions to reach it.

Personal Success Strategic Plan (PSSP)

DNA of Successful People
[5 minutes]

We all have goals we'd love to achieve, but the sad truth is that most of us will never achieve them. There have been plenty of studies done that show you how to achieve any goal. These studies illuminate what separates successful people from everyone else. But some people literally wander through life like player 2 and player 3 in our activity.

Think of three successful people and **write their names in your workbook on page 4**. The people you list could be politicians, entertainers, athletes, or even family members.

[Allow 30 seconds for participants to write down the three names.]

What do these individuals all have in common?

[Allow 1 minute for participants to discuss the commonalities of successful people.]

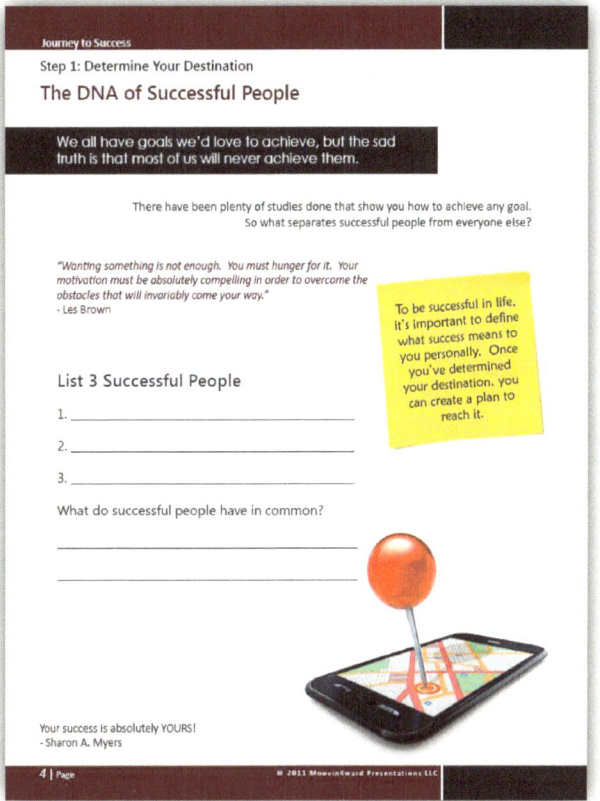

So here's the question. Based on what you listed, **do you possess what it takes to be successful?** *[Allow 20 seconds.]*

 **What separates high achievers from everyone else isn't ability or resources. It's hunger.**

Les Brown tells us, "Wanting something is not enough. You must hunger for it. Your motivation must be absolutely compelling in order to overcome the obstacles that will invariably come your way.'

These individuals have a hunger to succeed is so great that it fuels them to follow through and to keep fighting no matter what circumstances they face.

They don't get discouraged when their faith is tested. They know that doubt is a virus of the mind. They absolutely never entertain it. Instead, they quickly disregard it whenever it pays them a visit.

They are resilient enough to persist and keep on following through despite what their fears might tell them.

Getting Hungry

So how do you reach a state of hunger for YOUR success?

 **You need to want your success so badly that you'll perform at high output even when your faith is tested and there are no signs of success. And you need to be afraid of how uncomfortable you will be if you don't achieve your goal.**

When you have these internal motivations driving you, then all you need is a well-crafted PSSP that outlines all the steps you need to follow.

Increase Your Chances of Success

The Law of Attraction says that whatever you focus on and give your attention to, you attract more of into your life. What you think, talk, fantasize and worry about is what you'll manifest.

By having a PSSP, you're forced to put your focus and attention on your goals every single day. You can increase your chances of success when your success is planned, and you understand the true meaning of success.

True Meaning of Success

[5 minutes]

So what is the true meaning of success? **On page 5,** let's answer these questions together.

[Ask the following questions and allow time for responses]

- What is the social definition of success?

- How do you personally define success? What will success look like for you 20 years from now?

- How does *your* definition of success differ from *society's* definition of success?

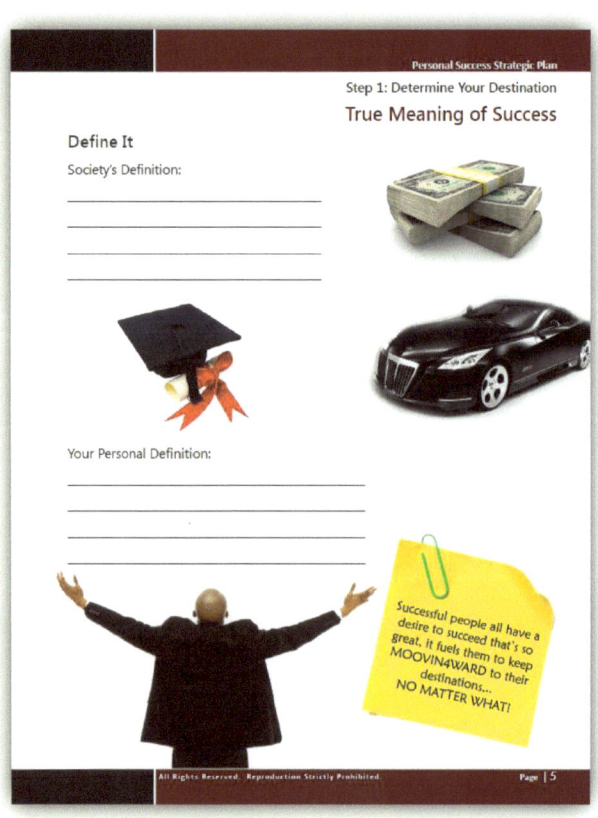

Keep in mind that it is perfectly fine that your definition matches or doesn't match society's definition. The point here is that it's YOUR definition that you're trying to attain.

 **A personal success strategic plan is critical if you want to achieve your personally defined true meaning of success**.

Why? Because achieving goals requires transformation on a mental and physical level, and a plan helps with managing resistance to change, which naturally arises when you make any significant shifts in your life.

People often begin setting goals without a solid destination of what they ultimately want to achieve. But if you don't have a destination in mind, then you'll never know which road to take to get where you want to go. Your destination needs to be clear—something you can visualize and describe to others. Without a clear view of what you want in life, you'll be forever changing course and falling short of your potential.

Now we've covered the first step of the PSSP, which is... *[Allow participants to state "Determine your Destination."]*

Let's move to Step 2.

Journey to Success Program

Step #2: Identify Your Purpose

It All Starts with You
[20 minutes]

In life, we think we know where we want to go… our success. But when our success doesn't match our purpose, we tend to encounter numerous roadblocks and don't quite understand why.

Imagine you want to become an architect because your family has always told you that you were a great artist, a prerequisite for becoming an architect. So they say. After years of college, you determine that your purpose in life is to help motivate children through art. While your destination was associated with art, becoming an architect was not your purpose in life.

You can significantly increase the odds of success in any endeavor, if you know who you are, what you want, where you are going, how you will get there, and what you will do once you arrive.

Follow along in your workbook on page 6 as we seek to understand the "questions" that provide us with the "answers" that summarize WHO YOU ARE. Let's start with your personal philosophy.

1. Personal Philosophy

Every person has a personal philosophy, consisting of some rules adopted from one's parents, culture, religion, environment, and so on. **On page 6 are some examples.**

- Not consuming meats and becoming a vegetarian
- When and how you worship, if at all
- Not to smoke cigarettes
- How you care for pets
- Using products made of animals
- Using only recycled materials

Generally speaking, these rules are not always well thought out and contain a wealth of inconsistencies and contradictions.

Your personal philosophy answers the question, "What do I believe?"

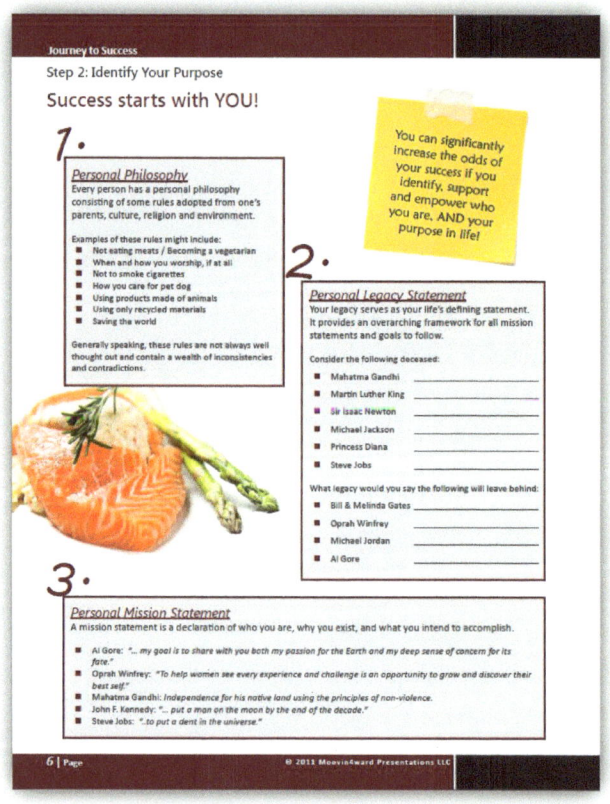

Personal Success Strategic Plan (PSSP)

In your **workbook on page 8**, write two of your personal philosophies. *[Allow 2 minutes.]*

2. Legacy Statement

Your legacy serves as your life's defining statement. It provides an overarching framework for all mission statements and goals to follow.

Turn back to page 6. Consider the following deceased. What were their legacies?

[Allow time for responses to each.]

- Mahatma Gandhi – *[peace, non-violence]*
- Martin Luther King – *[equality, civil rights, non-violence]*
- Steve Jobs – *[innovation, technology]*
- Michael Jackson – *[pop music, dance]*
- Princess Diana – *[charity]*

What legacy would you say the following *will* leave behind?
- Bill & Melinda Gates
- Oprah Winfrey
- Lebron James

Your legacy statement answers the question, "What do I want to be remembered for?"

In your **workbook on page 8**, write a quick draft legacy statement. *[Allow 2 minutes.]*

3. Mission Statement

A mission statement is a declaration of who you are, why you exist, and what you intend to accomplish. You can't exactly choose what legacy you leave behind, but you can choose what you want to achieve in your life that will contribute to the legacy you leave behind. Look at the list on **the bottom of page 6.**

- Al Gore: *"… my goal is to share with you both my passion for the Earth and my deep sense of concerned for its fate."*
- Oprah Winfrey: *"To help women see every experience and challenge is an opportunity to grow and discover their best self."*
- Charles Schwab: *"… to help everyone be financially fit."*
- John F. Kennedy: *"… put a man on the moon by the end of the decade."*

Your mission statement answers the question, "What do I want to achieve?"

In your **workbook on page 8**, write a draft mission statement. *[Allow 2 minutes.]*

Journey to Success Program

4. Core Values

Our values act as our compass, guiding us through life's terrain. Values represent an individual's highest priorities and deeply held driving forces that motivate our actions. In other words, we make choices based on our values. **Look at the examples at the top of page 7.**

Examples of values:

■ Ambition	■ Courage	■ Honesty
■ Competency	■ Wisdom	■ Innovativeness
■ Individuality	■ Independence	■ Teamwork
■ Equality	■ Security	■ Excellence
■ Integrity	■ Challenge	■ Accountability
■ Service	■ Influence	■ Empowerment
■ Responsibility	■ Learning	■ Quality
■ Accuracy	■ Compassion	■ Efficiency
■ Respect	■ Friendliness	■ Dignity
■ Dedication	■ Discipline/order	■ Collaboration
■ Diversity	■ Generosity	■ Stewardship
■ Improvement	■ Persistence	■ Empathy
■ Enjoyment/fun	■ Optimism	■ Accomplishment
■ Loyalty	■ Dependability	■ Credibility
■ Achievement	■ Advancement	■ Adventure
■ Pleasure	■ Power and Authority	■ Privacy
■ Public Service	■ Purity	■ Growth
■ Change and Variety	■ Community	■ Recognition
■ Knowledge	■ Stability	■ Appreciation
■ Democracy	■ Wealth	■ Reputation

So how do you know which are most important to you? We can all glance at this list and feel as though most are equally important. So let's do a quick exercise to help.

Activity 2.1: My Values

Time: 5 minutes

Materials: Participant workbook, page 7

Process:

On page 7, I want you to put a square around your 15 must have values. This won't be easy, but make your best effort. *[Allow about 60 seconds. Begin calling out a few of the values and providing examples. Some participants will need to understand the values in context.]*

Now of those 15 in squares, put a star by the 8 that are very important to your well-being. *[Allow another 60 seconds. Participants will begin to grumbling about the difficulty of the task. Motivate them through it.]*

> Of those 8 with stars, which four would you give up? Cross those out. *[Allow 30 seconds.]*
>
> Of the four remaining, circle the two that you could not live without. These are the ones that drive your action. They are your highest priorities and driving forces.

Your core values answer the question, "What is important to me?"

Back on **page 8 in your workbook**, list your top two core values. *[Allow 1 minute.]*

5. Code of Ethics

Lastly, on **the bottom on page 7,** let's look at Ethics.

Ethics are a personal code of behavior. For the most part they will help define what you do with your life, the career you choose, whether you have a family, whether you marry, whether you become a CEO, or … well, you get the picture.

That's because who you are defines your ethics and your ethics define who you are. It is a joined circle. Codes of conduct, personal creeds, and pledges all reflect an effort to make sense of things, to organize behavior, and to better understand ourselves.

Your future and the future of our world depend on how you behave.

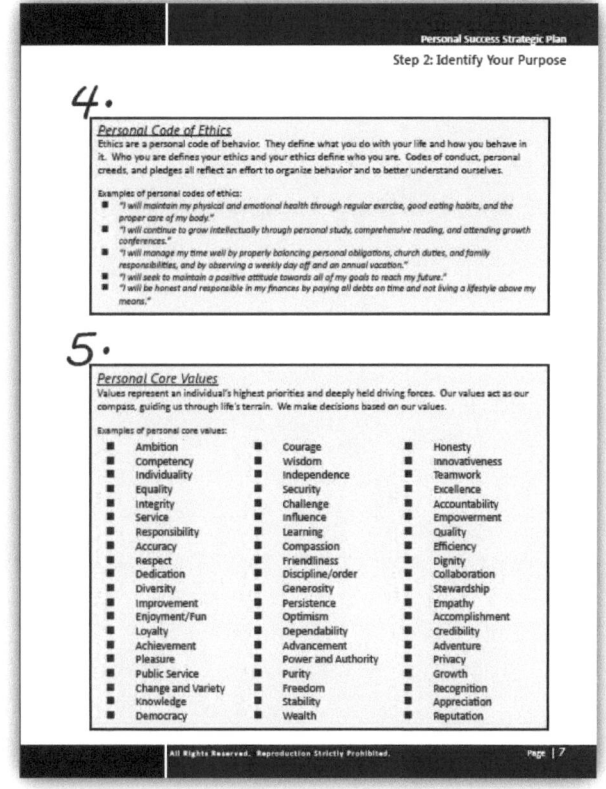

Examples of personal codes of ethics:
- "I will maintain my physical and emotional health through regular exercise, good eating habits, and the proper care of my body."
- "I will continue to grow intellectually through personal study, comprehensive reading, and attending growth conferences."
- "I will manage my time well by properly balancing personal obligations and family responsibilities, and by observing a weekly day off and an annual vacation."
- "I will be honest and responsible in my finances by paying all debts on time and not living a lifestyle above my means."

Journey to Success Program

Your code of ethics answers the question, "How will I live my life?"

On **page 8 in your workbook**, list two of your personal codes of ethics. *[Allow 2 minutes.]*

So let's review this summary on page 8.

Your answers to all of these questions provide fuel for achievement, and are the reasons behind all of your actions and inactions.

There is considerable evidence to indicate that your expectations of the future tend to shape your future. It seems reasonable, then, to spend some time determining specific, worthwhile expectations that will make your life more meaningful.

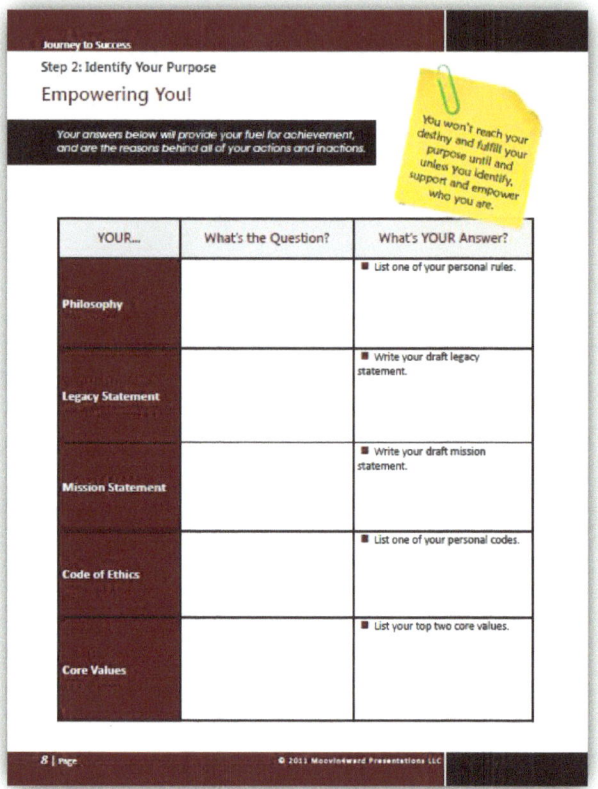

> **Key Concept**
> *You won't reach your destiny and fulfill your purpose until and unless you identify, support and empower who you are. .*

Purpose for Living

[5 minutes]

Deep within your consciousness is the realization that your life has a purpose, a destiny, a meaning to be discovered. To be working for a greater purpose, a purpose larger than you, is one of the secrets of making life significant.

Turn to page 9 in your workbook. Take a few moments to answer the two questions at the top of the page.

[Allow 3 minutes for participants to self-reflect to answer the questions, then discuss as a group.]

 **Successful people know what they want, how and when they will achieve it, but most importantly they know WHY they want to become successful at achieving their goals.**

Purpose Statement

Now that we have somewhat identified who you are and your purpose in life, we can now more effectively write our purpose statement. A purpose statement is a critical part of your PSSP.

What exactly is a purpose statement?

A **_purpose statement_** is a sentence capturing what you're driven to be in this lifetime; it is an image of the future that you want to bring into existence.

To craft your purpose statement, you should give yourself enough time to create a statement that will really mean something. Developing your purpose can take days, weeks or sometimes even months.

Remember, you're developing this to inspire you, so make sure it is positive, upbeat and energizes you. Ideally, you want this to become an internal mantra that guides your behavior and response to every action and circumstance you face, so keep it short and sharp, up to a maximum of four sentences.

In **your workbook on page 9,** take the next three minutes to draft a purpose statement.

[Allow 2 minutes.]

Once you have finalized your statement, you will ideally memorize it and use it to guide the formation of the rest of your PSSP, including your annual and monthly goals.

Consider writing your purpose statement on an index card and carry it in your wallet. Or stick a copy on your bathroom mirror. Become familiar with this thought as the principle that guides your life to your future.

Now we've covered the second step of the PSSP, let's review.

What was Step 1? *[Wait for participants to state, "Determine Your Destination."]*

What is Step 2? *[Wait for participants to state, "Identify Your Purpose."]*

Now let's talk about setting goals.

Workshop Script
Session 2: Goals & Strategies

Step #3: Set Your Goals

[5 minutes]

As the cliché goes, if you don't know where you're going, how will you ever know if you arrived? In addition to knowing your purpose in life, you also need to set goals to help you get where you want to go in life.

A **_Goal_** is something that someone wants to achieve and is an important fundamental element to developing a sound PSSP.

Why is goal setting important anyway? How else can you hope to achieve your true meaning of success? Goal setting helps you to develop motivation and forces you to focus your time and energy.

When you lack goals, it's difficult to avoid just drifting through life as your day-to-day decisions have no larger purpose. Hence the saying, "If you aren't sure where you're going, any road will lead you there."

Your purpose statement is different from your goals. Your goals are your _short-term_ desires that drive you to take specific and planned actions.

Your purpose statement is much bigger and more _long-term_. In fact, it's what enables you to stay focused on your goals and helps you avoid getting side-tracked.

For example:
A short-term goal might be to:
- Finish school
- Move into a new residence
- Break-up with the person I'm dating

A long-term goal might be to:
- Become President of the US
- Visit 20 foreign countries
- Marry the person I'm dating and have three children

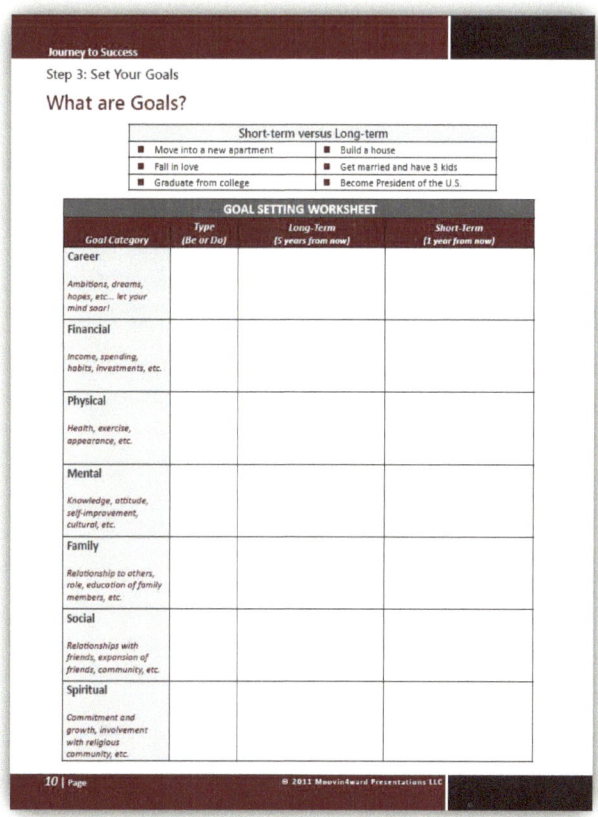

Activity 3.1: Goal Setting Worksheet

Time: 10 minutes

Materials: Student Workbook page 10

Process:

Let's try a quick exercise to get your thoughts flowing on the short and long-term goals that you have in various areas of your life. **On page 10** in your workbook, is a Goal Setting Worksheet.

Take some time to fill in at least one goal for four of the areas listed. It looks tough, but you can do it. This will hopefully help you to better understand the differences between long-term and short-term goals.

As you can see, this worksheet lists the following goal categories: career, financial, physical, mental, family, social and spiritual. While this is more than will be required for your PSSP, we are using this exercise as practice for goal setting. Complete this independently—these are **your** goals. I'll keep you posted of the time so that you can get through all of them.

[Explain each category. Inform participants of the time after 2 minutes for career goals, 1 minute for financial, 1 minute for physical, 1 minute for mental, 1 minute for family, and 1 minute for social, and 1 minute for spiritual (total time is 8 minutes).]

Who would like to share with the group?

[Allow 2 minutes for participant discussion. Be sure to touch each category.

Categories of Goals

When it comes to goals, there are two categories: "be" goals and "do" goals.

In other words, who do you want to BE or what do you want to DO? Within each category, there are four areas of goals: wealth, health, relationships, and self-fulfillment. So any goal you set for yourself will fall into one of these areas.

When a business professional sets a goal, it tends to be either a wealth goal or a relationship goal. However, achievement involves all four areas, and success means finding balance in the four areas.

In order to live a successful life, you need both "being" and "doing" goals in each of the four areas.

Go **back to page 10** and list a BE or DO goal for at least four of the areas.

[Allow 2 minutes.]

Who is willing to share?

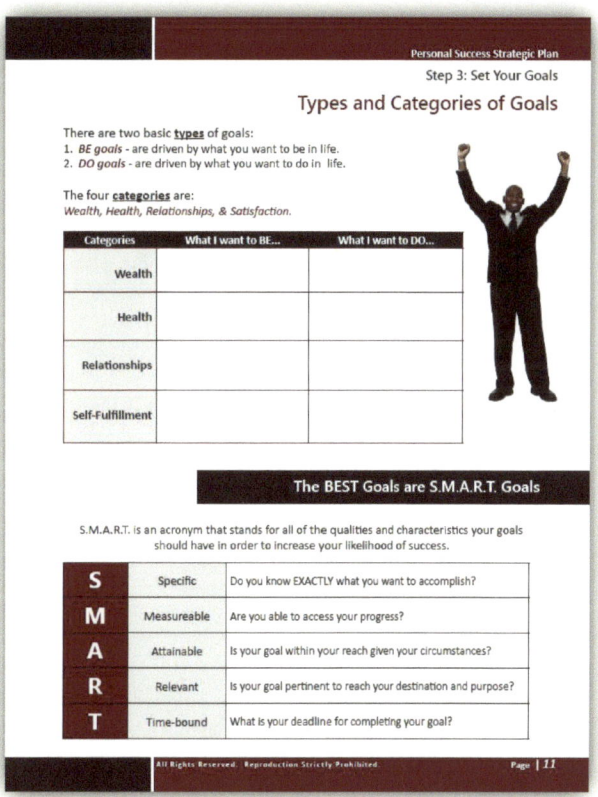

Set SMART Goals

[5 minutes]

Now that you know why having goals is important, you need to understand that not just any goal will do. We want to be sure that we set SMART goals. *[Have someone read the acronym for S.M.A.R.T.]*

 **SMART is an acronym that stands for all of the qualities and characteristics your goals should have in order to increase your likelihood of success.**

When your goals are written following the SMART system, it's easier to practice positive thinking.

In truth, we are all so resistant to change that we often try to sabotage our success. We will not allow ourselves enough time or we'll not be specific enough in how we set our goals. Often we do this unconsciously and then end up failing and feel perplexed as to why.

So what are SMART goals exactly? SMART is a system or a framework for judging the components of your goal. It stands for:

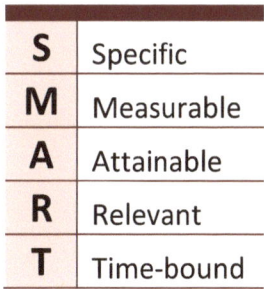

Let's review each of these attributes. **Please take notes on page 11 of your workbook.**

Specific

Do you know exactly what you want to accomplish?

To achieve a goal, you need to be specific about what it is. Otherwise it's difficult to turn your vision into set tasks. To be specific, your goal should state clearly what you intend to accomplish. This will allow you to know exactly what you're working toward.

- *Bad example: "I want to become healthier."*
- *Good example: "I want to become healthier by changing my diet to replace junk food with fruits and increase my workouts to three times a week."*

Measurable

Are you able to assess your progress?

Making a goal measurable makes it possible to monitor your progress. It also forces you to become clear on where you're starting from, which is always important. If your goal is too undefined, you'll find it's impossible to tell when you have even achieved it. Your goal is measurable if you are 100% clear what success will look like and what failure will look like.

- *Bad example: "I want to be rich."*
- *Good example: "I want to generate a quarter of a million dollars in liquid income within 10 years from today."*

Attainable

Is your goal within your reach given your current situation?

Research has shown that one of the most important elements of success is having a goal that's achievable. It's easy to get caught up wanting to do something HUGE. But the problem is: it's difficult to stay motivated over the long run if your goal seems unattainable. You will easily feel hopeless and abandon your efforts.

To ensure your goal will motivate you, break a really large goal down into smaller ones. At the same time, you don't want your goal to seem too small. The best size is one that stretches you without breaking you.

- *Bad example: "I want to become a millionaire in 2 months."*
- *Good example: "I want to become a millionaire within 10 years by starting my own business and winning government contracts to provide services in warzone countries."*

Relevant

Is your goal pertinent towards your destination and purpose in life?

A goal is relevant if it elevates you to your larger goals, your overall purpose. Remember that your goals are intended to help you reach your ultimate destination, and therefore should not divert you from that achievement.

Let's say that your long term goal is to purchase a home and it will take you five years to save the down payment. But in the short-term, you decide to take a two-week vacation in Las Vegas with friends, which will use up two years of your savings. It seems that your short-term goal is in conflict with your bigger vision.

- *Bad example: "After I earn my degree in agriculture, I want to become a rap star."*
- *Good example: "Before I graduate with my degree in agriculture, I want to work an internship with a large company in the agriculture industry."*

Time Bound

What is the deadline for completing your goal?

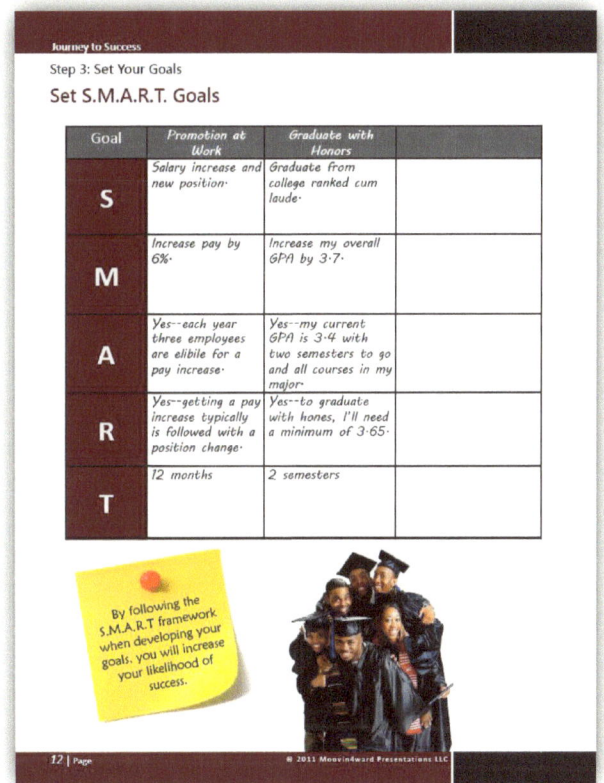

Deadlines are critical. They keep you in action and they keep you motivated. Without a time limit there's no urgency to start taking action now.

Make sure you are realistic with your time frame. There's nothing less motivating than missing your goal all because you didn't allow yourself the right amount of time.

- *Bad example: "I am going to work on my project."*
- *Good example: "I am going to finish my project by Sunday evening at 8pm and I'll achieve this by working six hours on Saturday evening and six hours on Sunday afternoon."*

Make sure that you follow the SMART framework when developing your goals and you'll increase your likelihood of success.

So let's give it a try. **Turn to page 12 of your workbook**. Notice that we have two goals already listed with the SMART actions. *[Depending upon your audience, review the example that best applies. Then allow 5 minutes for participants to select a goal and identify the SMART actions that might apply. Ask for volunteers to share their results.]*

Goal setting allows us to be proactive, instead of just being reactive. Goal setting is just the first step to achievement.

Step #4: Develop Your Strategy

Remember that goals need a plan of action.

Imagine, for instance, that your goal is to get an internship position. Knowing that your goal has to be SMART, you list that you want to get an internship position for a company based in Washington, DC by the summer of your junior year. Sounds SMART.

Time passes. May of your junior year rolls around and you don't have an internship position. While you started out well, by setting a SMART goal to achieve, *you didn't perform any action to help you achieve the goal.*

What's missing from this scenario is a strategy to help you accomplish the goal you have set. You didn't register with the career development office; that's a strategy. You didn't search for or submit any applications; those are strategies.

Not having a strategy is like trying to pin the tail on a donkey when you're blindfolded. You don't have a chance.

<u>Your strategy is simply your plan of action that you will execute to accomplish your goals.</u>

What will you do to make success a reality based on the goals you've set?

In selecting your strategies, make sure they are suitable for the goal you are trying to accomplish. Your intent is to develop a plan of action that will allow you to achieve your goal.

If your strategies are not appropriate and suitable for the goals you are trying to achieve, then YOU'LL FAIL! For example, if your goal is to lose 25 pounds and your strategy is to stop eating, you will more than likely fail or starve to death trying.

You should also ensure that the strategies you choose are appropriate for YOU. There is likely more than one way to do something, but what works for others might not work for you.

To increase your likelihood of developing strategies that will help you to achieve your goals, you'll need to create a Personal SWOT Analysis (PSA).

Personal SWOT Analysis

[5 minutes]

To develop your strategies, it's important to fully understand what makes you tick. Therefore, you need to understand the internal and external environmental factors that affect you.

With that understanding, you can develop strategies that highlight your clear advantages and use those to be successful. From there, you can make informed choices and implement your strategy effectively.

First, what is a SWOT analysis? **Turn to page 13 in your workbooks.**

It is a strategic planning method used to evaluate the **S**trengths, **W**eaknesses, **O**pportunities, and **T**hreats of a project, endeavor or person. Businesses use a SWOT Analysis to help develop strategies to accomplish business goals and achieve success, based on the capabilities and resources of the company.

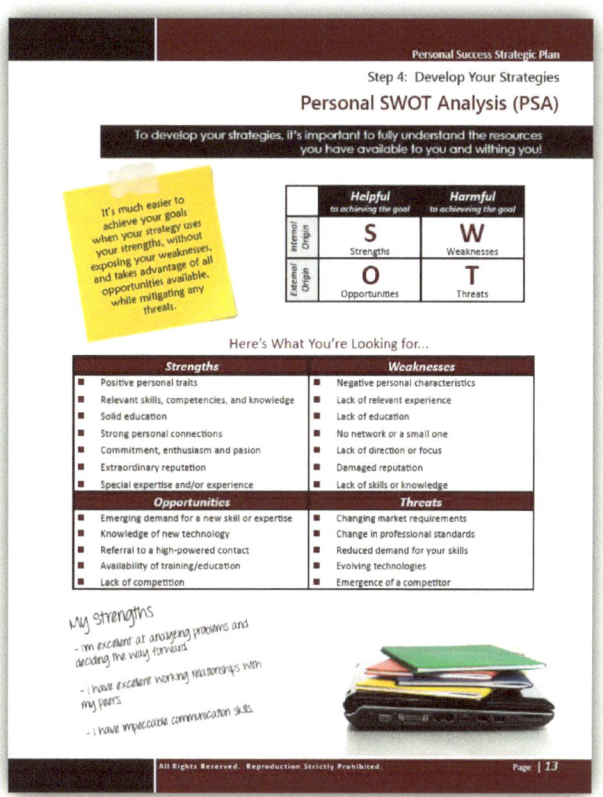

Developing Your PSA

Your PSA is a great tool for uncovering what you personally do well and where you have weaknesses. It's much easier to achieve your goals when your strategy uses your strengths without exposing your weaknesses and takes advantage of all opportunities available.

Once you've completed your PSA, take time to think about the different things you could do to create a clear advantage to meet your goals. **Brainstorm** on ideas then eliminate those that don't take advantage of your strengths. You'll also want to brainstorm on ways to maximize your opportunities, minimize your threats, and perhaps even turn your threats into opportunities.

With your destination in mind and the goals you have set in front of you, think about the possible actions you could take in order to achieve those goals. After an overview of each quadrant of the PSA, you'll have opportunity to begin brainstorming for your own.

Internal: Strengths & Weaknesses

The top two sections (STRENGTHS and WEAKNESSES) both originate internally. These are things that you can control. Strengths are helpful, weaknesses are harmful.

Strengths

Strengths are your internal, positive attributes and selling points. Develop a list of your capabilities and resources that can be used to help you achieve your goals. Then ask yourself, *"What are my most important strengths? How can I best use my strengths to help me move forward?"*

Here's what you're looking for:

- Positive personal traits
- Relevant skills, competencies, knowledge and work experience
- A solid education
- Strong personal connections
- Commitment, enthusiasm and passion for your field
- Extraordinary reputation
- Special expertise and/or experience

Weaknesses

Next, develop a list of areas that need improvement. Weaknesses can sometimes be the absence of certain strengths, and in some cases, a weakness may be the reverse side of your strength. Ask yourself, *"What areas do I need to improve? How can I overcome my weaknesses?"*

Here's what you're looking for:

- Negative personal characteristics
- A lack of relevant experience
- A lack of education
- No network or a small one
- A lack of direction or focus
- Damaged reputation
- Lack of skills or knowledge

External: Threats & Opportunities

The lower two sections (OPPORTUNITIES and THREATS) both originate externally. These are things that you cannot control. Things that are happening around you that may affect the outcome of your efforts to achieve your goals. Opportunities are helpful; threats are harmful.

Opportunities

Opportunities are external events that you can potentially take advantage of. In addition to new or significant trends, what other external opportunities exist and how can we best benefit from those. Ask yourself, ***"What trends are in my favor? What's going on in the world that can benefit me?"***

Here's what you're looking for:

- Favorable industry trends
- A booming economy
- A specific job opening
- An upcoming company project
- Emerging demand for a new skill or expertise
- Use of new technology
- Referral to a high-powered contact
- Availability of training/education
- Lack of competition

Threats

These are anything that can stand in the way of your success. No one is immune to threats, but too many people miss, ignore or minimize these threats, often at great cost or time loss. Ask yourself, ***"What can I do to eliminate each threat? Can a threat become an opportunity?"***

Here's what you're looking for:

- Industry restricting and consolidation
- Changing market requirements
- Changing professional standards that you don't' meet
- Reduced demand for one of your skills
- Evolving technologies you're unprepared for
- The emergence of a competitor

Activity 4.1: Completing Your PSA

Time: 10 minutes

Materials: Student Workbook pages 14-17

Process:

Let's take some time now to brainstorm on your PSA. **Turn to page 14** in your workbook.

We'll start with your strengths. Begin by listing a few of your most important strengths. List only those strengths that will benefit you and move you towards your life goals. *[Allow 3 minutes.]*

Let's now work on your weaknesses. Be very honest with your assessment of yourself. How can these weaknesses hinder you from reaching your goals? *[Allow 3 minutes.]*

Next, **on page 15** list any opportunities that might exist and why these opportunities will help you to reach your goal. *[Allow 2 minutes.]*

Lastly, list any threats that may get in the way. How can these threats hinder your success? Be sure to be as specific as possible. *[Allow 2 minutes.]*

Now let's use this information to fill in your PSA **on page 16.** We don't have enough time to really delve deep into your responses, so consider coming back to these later to review and refine. You might even consider having someone close to you to provide you with feedback.

On page 17 are examples, both in "brainstorming" and "complete sentence" format.

Keep in mind that the intent of this process is to help you to understand your skills, attributes and experiences that you can use to your advantage.

Personal Success Strategic Plan (PSSP)

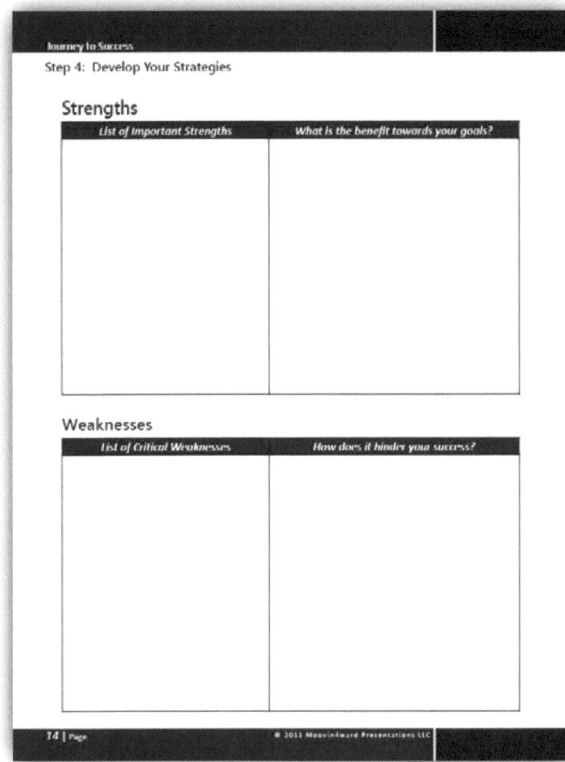
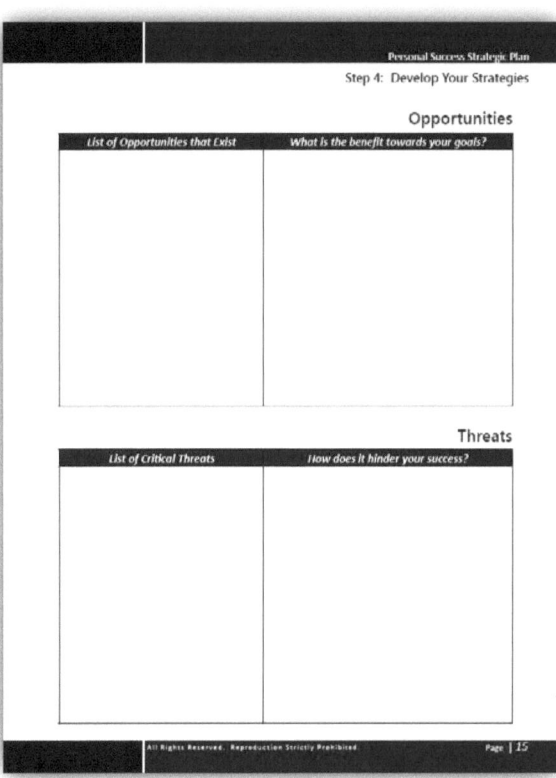
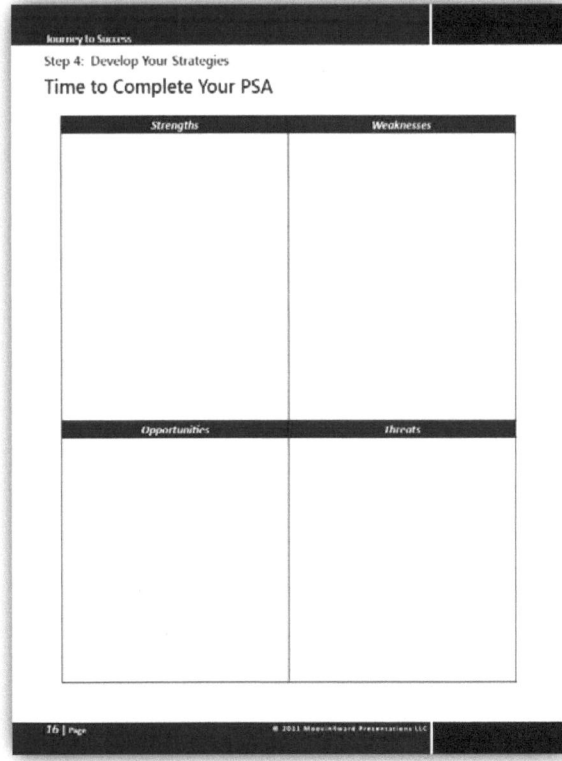
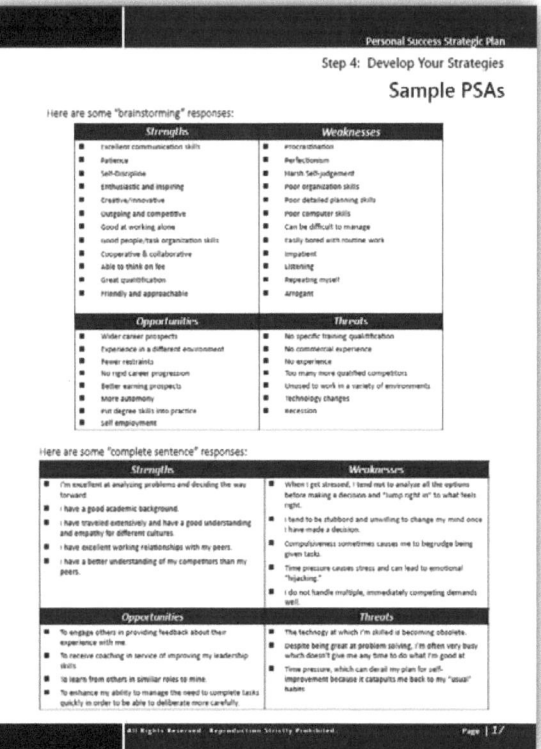

Journey to Success Program

Developing Strategies

[5 minutes]

Now that you have your PSA, you can use this information to develop the suitable strategies to achieve the goals you set. By suitable, we want to make sure that the strategy is appropriate.

For example, if you wanted to earn a degree in less than four years, skipping classes and/or interning would not be suitable strategies for your goal. If your goal is to land a job immediately after college, interning would be perfect strategy to achieve your goal.

Keep in mind that your strategy is your plan of action. How will you make it happen?

Has anyone ever played chess? *[Raise your hand]*

So what is the goal or objective of chess? *["To capture the king of the opponent."]*

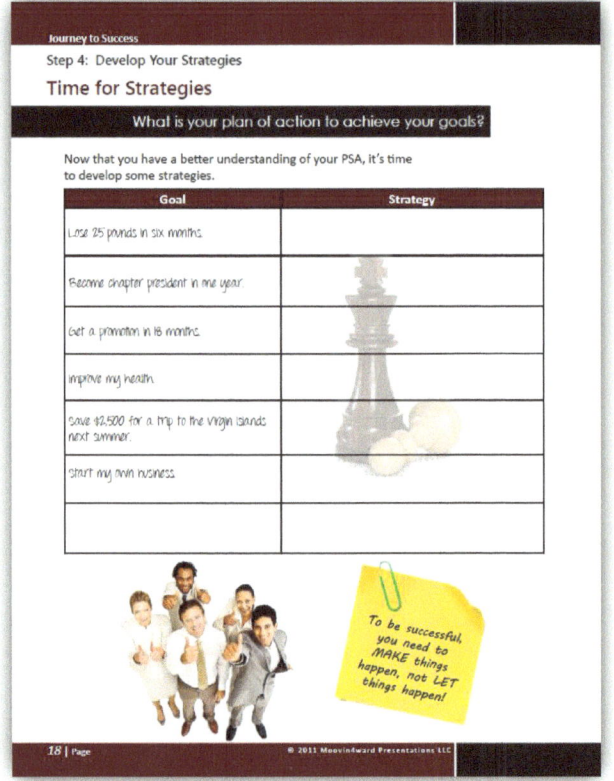

What are the strategies used to reach this goal? *[Allow responses and thank the participants.]*

You start these games with this plan of action in mind. Typically, it's a bit more than just "winning," it is *how* you'll win.

Turn to page 18 in your workbook. Here we have several goals listed. Let's walk thru them.

Let's say you have a SMART goal to lose 25 pounds in six months. What strategies or plan of action might you take to achieve your goal? *[We are looking for "change your diet, exercise regularly, fasting", etc.]*

Excellent. Let's try another one. Let's say you have just joined a new student organization on campus and your goal is to become chapter president by the next year. What strategies might you take to achieve your goal? *[We are looking for "actively participate, review the requirements in the bylaws, start campaigning, track your contributions", etc.]*

Good job!

Personal Success Strategic Plan (PSSP)

Activity 4.2: Plan of Action

Time: 10 minutes

Materials: Student Workbook pages 19

Process:

Now select a partner from someone sitting close to you and come up with some strategies for two of the other goals listed in your workbook on page 18. We'll discuss these together in about 3 minutes.

[After 2 minutes take a few suggestions for each goal to discuss as a group for about 3 minutes.]

Now turn to page 19. With your partner, I'd like you to list three of the goals that you created earlier and come up with a strategy for each.

Understand that most goals require a variety of strategies, but we're only listing a primary strategy for this exercise. You'll have 3 minutes to work on it.

[After 3 minutes, ask for volunteers to share their goal and strategy. Discuss as many as you can for about 2 minutes.]

To be successful, you need to make things happen, not just let things happen.

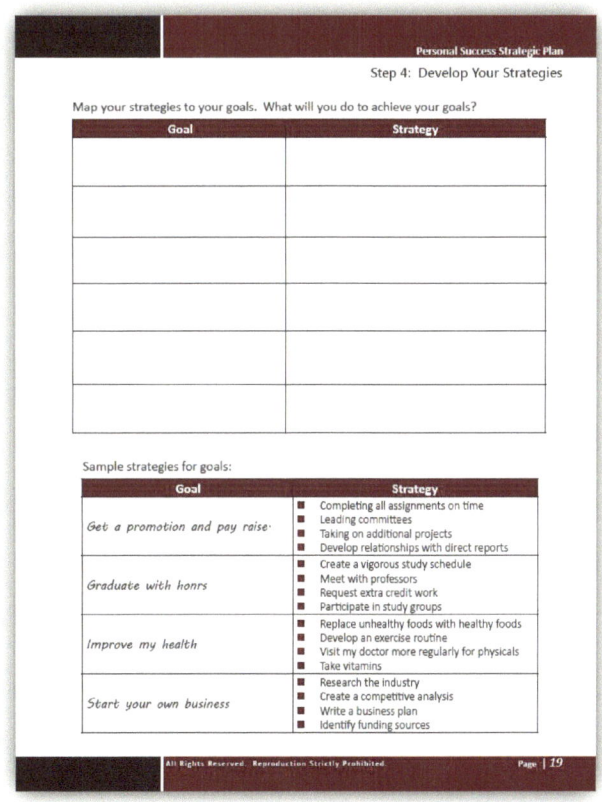

We've now covered the fourth step of the PSSP, let's review.

What was Step 1? *[Wait for participants to state, "Determine Your Destination."]*

What is Step 2? *[Wait for participants to state, "Identify Your Purpose."]*

What is Step 3? *[Wait for participants to state "Set Your Goals."]*

What is Step 4? *[Wait for participants to state "Develop Your Strategies."]*

Time to take action!

Workshop Script
Session 3: Action & Progress

Step # 5: Take Action

Now it's time to get moving; time to take action and make it happen. There are three key components needed to get you going. You must have a **positive attitude**, be **self-motivated**, and **work hard**. You need to have and maintain these qualities in order to persevere to your final destination.

Positive Attitude

[2 minutes]

Let's start with a Positive Attitude. There are so many benefits of a positive attitude.

For starters, a positive attitude will give you a heightened sense of well being and it will help cure any self esteem problem you might have.

But that's only the beginning. Read any book by Jack Canfield or Bob Proctor and you'll quickly learn that the quality of your attitude dictates what you can attract into your life. Esther and Jerry Hicks sum it up nicely in their book *Money and The Law of Attraction:* **"There is nothing more detrimental to your ability to positively attract than a negative attitude toward yourself."**

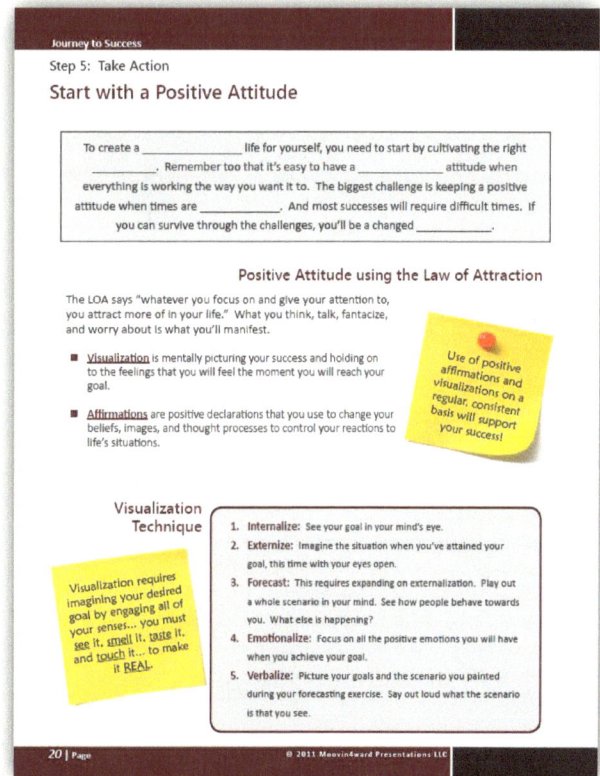

-So if you're wondering why that thing you really want just won't make its way into your life despite the fact you have a plan in place to attract it, consider it's your attitude that's blocking the way.

Considering the many benefits of a positive attitude, why aren't more people positive? The reality is that we are socialized to be cynical and lazy.

We're programmed to blame everyone else (especially our parents!) for all that's going wrong in our lives. We seek out jobs that will give us the highest pay for the least amount of work, never considering what will lead to satisfaction and happiness.

Most people think they have a positive attitude. But many don't. Someone who uses the power of a positive attitude isn't swayed by negative circumstances. They see them as minor speed bumps in their journey.

Take a few moments to fill in the blanks at the top of page 20. I have a prize for the first person to complete it correctly. You have one minute. *[Start your clock and/or wait for the first hand. The correct answers are highlighted below. Be sure to reiterate the proper response.]*

Success Starts With a Positive Attitude

If you are serious about creating a successful life for yourself, you need to start by cultivating the right attitude. Whether or not you have a positive attitude right now, you can adopt one. Remember, a positive attitude isn't a feeling. It's a state of mind. You develop a positive attitude by *deciding* you'll respond positively to life circumstances, no matter what.

> **Fill in the Blanks:**
> *To create a **successful** life for yourself, you need to start by cultivating the right **attitude**. Remember too that it's easy to have a **positive** attitude when everything is working the way you want to. The biggest challenge is keeping a positive attitude when times are **difficult**. And most success will require difficult times. If you can survive through the challenges, you'll be a changed **person**.*

There will be days when it's difficult to maintain a positive attitude, but don't be discouraged. What separates high achievers from everybody else is their ability to regain their positive attitude after they have fallen off the wagon. Be sure you get right back on again.

Most importantly, resolve to start right now to be more positive. Always look for *how* you can do something rather than *why* you can't. Believe in yourself no matter what. And be disciplined enough to continuously seek ways to improve. If you do this diligently, in time you will start to experience the truly life-changing benefits of a positive attitude.

Law of Attraction

[3 minutes]

On Feb 3, 1987, the New York Times published a research report on the power of positive thinking. On that report Edward E Jones, a psychologist at Princeton University said, "Our expectancies not only affect how we see reality but also affect the reality itself".

The Law of Attraction (LOA) says that whatever you focus on and give your attention to; you attract more of in your life. What you think, talk, fantasize, and worry about is what you'll manifest.

The most important part of the law of attraction is that you always need to think positive and believe in your goals without having any doubts in your mind.

Creative visualization and affirmation in achieving goals are the two most popular techniques used by many people and recommended by the masters of LOA.

Visualization Techniques

Success begins within and visualization is a great way to convince yourself you can achieve your dreams. When you are trying to manifest your goals, you're essentially trying to change something about your current state of existence. And with any change, the mind resists as the ego perceives the unknown to be a threat to the balance that it maintains.

The first step of visualization is to find your goal and make an action plan to achieve it. You must take a few minutes of your day to imagine that you have achieved your goal.

Try to take a mental picture of the day of your success and hold on to the feelings that you will feel the moment you will reach your goal. Most importantly try to interact with the day of your success in your mind. Try to feel what it's like to have your friends congratulate you on your success.

Using Visualization

As human beings, we have a tendency to sabotage our own efforts. This is why it's important to incorporate visualization exercises into your daily PSSP. You only need to spend a few minutes in the morning and just before going to sleep, picturing your success.

We can all visualize, it just takes practice. Sometimes, until you get good at it, it may only be words or feelings that come to you. That's okay but the more you practice the easier it will become. Let me show you how well you can already visualize.

Please close your eyes. *[Make sure all or most have closed their eyes before you start. Then share the following description with the group or you can create and use your own visualization. Be sure that you include details that require all five senses: sight, smell, sound, taste, and touch.]*

> **Baking Cookies**
> *Imagine that you're going to a bakery to help make cookies. You walk into the bakery and the smell of fresh baked muffins and breads fill your nostrils. As you enter the kitchen, you feel the warmth from the industrial-sized heated ovens. You head over to the giant stainless steel refrigerator to get your ingredients and you feel the cool air on your face as you grab five pounds of butter and a dozen eggs. You close the door and head over to your workspace where the huge shinny stainless steel industrial mixer is waiting.*
>
> *With your measuring cup, you scoop a cup of flour from the bend to dump into your mixing bowl, the powders float up to your face and you fan away the cloud. You reach for two more cups to repeat the process. You unwrap the cool but slightly melted and mushy margarine and dump it into your mixing bowl.*
>
> *Next, you scoop a cup of brown sugar, which feels like wet sand when it touches your fingers. Next, you crack one egg at a time on the table and pour the slimy insides into*

your mixture. Crack, pour, crack, pour... you repeat this process over and over until you've used all of the eggs. During the process, you accidentally drop an egg shell in the mix. You reach into the mixture to retrieve the shell and you feel the slimy cold egg on your fingers.

Next, you add the vanilla extract. As soon as you open the bottle, the strong vanilla flavor hits you and almost knocks you out. You pour the needed amount into the mixture and now you're ready to blend.

You press the big green ON button on the mixer and it starts to loudly hum and rotate its blades, slowly mixing your batter. You stop the machine to pour in your honey and chocolate chips. You can't resist popping a chip in your mouth; oh the taste of chocolate. You start the machine again; it hums, and blends all of the ingredients into a smooth, creamy batter. With a big spoon, you lump moist dough drops onto your baking pan until all of the batter has been used and you've scrapped the remnants off the bowl.

Next, you open your preheated oven and the heat immediately moistens your face with steam. You put your cookie pan in the oven and set your timer for 15 minutes. After about 5 minutes you begin to smell the aroma of the vanilla, honey and brown sugar which makes your mouth water.

Moments later, BING, the timer alerts you that the cookies are ready. You open the oven and again the heat blows on your face. After you place the pan on the cooking rack, you are tempted to try one. You know that the cookie is hot, but you pick one up anyway, and drop it because it's actually too hot.

Seconds later you pick up the warm cookie which begins to fold around your fingers and you can see the melted chocolate spreading from the cookie. You lick your fingers and take a bite of the cookie. As it melts in your mouth your squeeze your eyes shut.

At this point, if you haven't already, you'll probably want to wipe your mouth. The idea of visualization is to see yourself in it. If this visualization worked correctly, you possibly felt that you could taste, smell, fell, see and hear every part of this small visualization.

That's how it works.

Creative Visualization

The more vivid you make it—in bright, living, moving, color—the better. For optimum results, use all five senses to work for you in reaching your desired goals. By combining the elements of sight, smell, sound, taste and touch to visualize your desired end-result, it becomes more real to your imagination and, as a result, becomes deeply embedded in your subconscious which, as discussed above, becomes your reality.

Understanding Affirmations

[5 minutes]

Affirmations are positive declarations used to control reactions to life's situations.

Creating an affirmation is the act of writing your desires or goals in positive sentences in present tense. This technique has tremendous power to affect our mind in achieving goals, because we are writing and reading them at the same time, so it's like a double hit of energy.

It works by delivering positive messages straight to your subconscious mind. If you repeat them regularly you can begin to reprogram your mind to have and maintain a positive thought pattern which helps attract your desires.

Affirmations are a useful tool to help change the beliefs, images and thought processes that you have within you. It is a "self-talk" that affirms you positively or negatively.

For example, how often have you said to yourself "No, I'm not good at…?" or "Yes, I can do this!" These are both affirmations, but affirmations that can either prevent you from moving forward to accomplishment or propel you.

Take a look on page 21.

There are three statements that shape positive self-talk
- **I AM** – a statement of who you are.
- **I CAN** – a statement of your potential.
- **I WILL** – a statement of positive change in your life.

I AM statements are positive affirmations of a real state of being that exists in you.
- ☑ I am competent.
- ☑ I am patient.
- ☑ I am forgiving.

I CAN statements are positive affirmations of your ability to accomplish goals.
- ☑ I can lose weight.
- ☑ I can let go of guilt.
- ☑ I can handle my course load.

I WILL statements are positive affirmations of a change you want to achieve.
- ☑ I will like myself better each day.
- ☑ I will graduate with honors.
- ☑ I will let go of past mistakes.

Using Affirmations

Affirmations are a way of starting and ending each day. By learning to consciously verbalize positive thoughts to ourselves, we will reap the benefits of positive thinking.

Using affirmations has impacted my life. *[Give your personal testimony as to how you have used affirmations.]*

Positive affirmation are a fundamental part of using the Law of Attraction, and anything that helps you to keep remembering and repeating your affirmation, you must use.

Crafting Affirmations

We discussed basic affirmations, but you can also create your own specific affirmation. Shelley Holmes, www.makeadentleadership.com, shares these 7 steps to crafting affirmations. Write these **in your workbook on page 21.**

1. **Be Clear About the Problem**

Many times people develop affirmations around the symptom of their problem, rather than going to the root cause. If you affirm a symptom, rather than the root cause of your problem, you may well find that you achieve results in the short term, but long term the results are not sustainable.

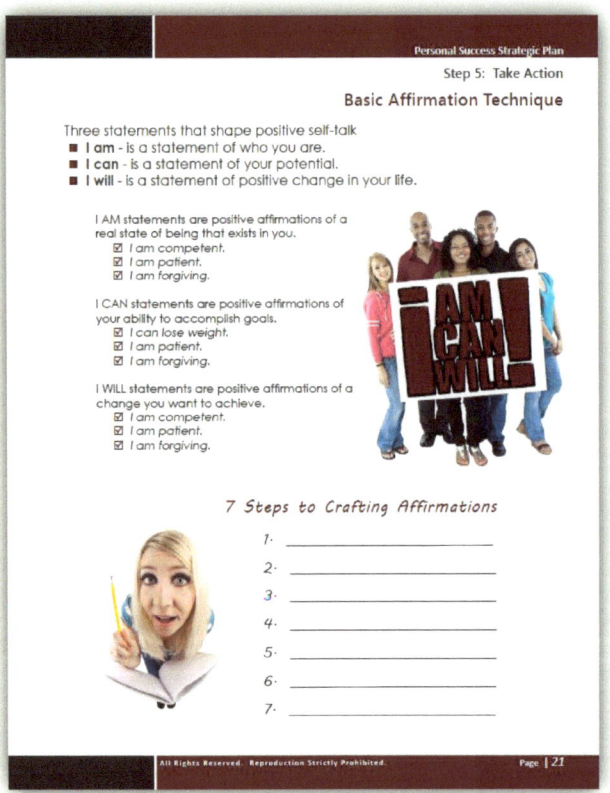

For example, you decide that you need a "graduate from college" affirmation, which is certainly achievable. But on a deeper level, the affirmation you really need is about going to class on time, completing assignments, staying on tasks, and studying properly. So you may actually need multiple affirmations and not just one to be clear.

As you begin to write your affirmations, ask yourself, "what is the real issue?" This may require a great deal of reflection, insight, and honesty.

2. **Use Present Tense**

Affirmations are more effective when stated in the present tense. For example; "*I love my wonderful job*" is a present tense affirmation. "I am going to love my job" is affirming something in the future tense, and even though it is only a subtle shift in the phrasing of the words, your subconscious, like an ipod, only records what you put in there.

Therefore, by affirming "I am going to ..." you may well find yourself waiting a very long time for the results to happen, because you are forever 'going to'. **Write the affirmation as if you have already achieved it.**

3. <u>**Make It About You**</u>

Your affirmation needs to be about you. **So it will always include either the word "I" or "me" in it.** You cannot make affirmations for other people.

For example you could not affirm: "My team members are open and honest with each other" - this affirmation will never change their behavior. However, if you were to say, "*I am open and honest with my team members acting as a role model to my team*", then you may well find that your personal change will, strangely enough, have a positive impact on and may lead to changes in those around you.

Other people, reading your affirmations, may think they sound very self-centered and selfish. And that is exactly how they are meant to be - this is a self-improvement project.

4. <u>**Add Emotions**</u>

E-motion=Energy in motion. The emotion fuels the energy to create the result i.e. if it doesn't get you excited; it is not a powerful affirmation. So, **get involved, be passionate, and use your emotions!** Use phrases like: *I am delighted, I am so excited, It is easy for me*, etc. Bring your spirit and energy in to the affirmation - the stronger the feeling an affirmation conveys, the deeper the impression it makes on your mind and the sooner you experience positive results.

5. <u>**Be Positive**</u>

Create affirmations in positive terms while avoiding negative statements. **Affirm what you do want, rather than what you do not want.** For example: "I am never sad or depressed." What pictures does this negative statement immediately bring to your mind? Negativity. Rather affirm, "*I have a positive and optimistic outlook on life*". This statement is much more powerful as it is positive and reinforces your desired goal.

The words that you use trigger in your mind emotions and feelings. You want these to be positive and uplifting. The quickest and easiest way to ensure that you write your affirmation in the positive is to identify what it is you don't want and then ask yourself the question: "What is it that I do want?" Write your affirmation from the answer you get to this question.

6. <u>**Be Specific & Brief**</u>

Short affirmations are easy to say, and have a far greater impact at a subconscious level than those that are long and wordy. **Keeping them specific and to the point adds power** as the idea is uncluttered by extraneous elements. If need be, have two or three affirmations around the one topic.

7. <u>**Be Visual**</u>

Now that you have written your affirmation, the key to manifesting what it is you want, is the process of vividly visualizing yourself as if you have already obtained your desired outcome. Your brain does not differentiate between vividly imagined events and real events. **Visualize often enough and with plenty of emotion attached and your brain thinks that this is real.**

This is great when we are plugging positive stuff into ourselves. Not so terrific when we are plugging negative stuff!

Activity 5.1: Affirmation Cards

Time: 5 minutes

Materials: Index cards

Process:

Pass out index cards to all participants.

I'm passing out index cards. In the next few minutes, write down an affirmation using the crafting steps that I've just shared. This affirmation should motivate you to reach your destination.

[Allow 5 minutes.]

Place them where you can see them daily and be reminded of positive aspects about you. Every time you see these cards, read your daily affirmation to remind yourself about your positive qualities and attributes.

At the **top of page 22**, you'll see two options for using affirmations.

Option #1 starts with this one card we just completed. You can create a total of 30 cards and re-read them each month. If you're really good, you can create 365 cards and re-read them year after year.

Option #2 uses sticky notes. You can write your affirmation on a note and stick them in various places, your bedroom, bathroom, kitchen, car, etc. This allows you to surround yourself with personal positivity.

 **Use of positive affirmations and visualizations on a regular and consistent basis will support your success.**

Let's connect the visualization & affirmation techniques to help achieve the goals you defined earlier in order to reinforce them.

Personal Success Strategic Plan (PSSP)

Activity 5.2: Visualization & Affirmation

Time: 5 minutes

Materials: Student Workbook page 22

Process:

In the first column, take a moment to describe what you see or visualize when you achieve this goal. *[Allow 2 minutes.]*

Keep in mind that success in each of these areas differs for all of us. Stick with what you see or visualize for you.

Now in the second column, take 2 more minutes to write down a strong affirmation to help you stay motivated to accomplish the goal. *[Allow 2 minutes.]*

The impact of our expectations is powerful. By using affirmations and visualizations, you control the outcome of your expectations.

We've seen that your expectations not only affect your daily performance, but your future as well.

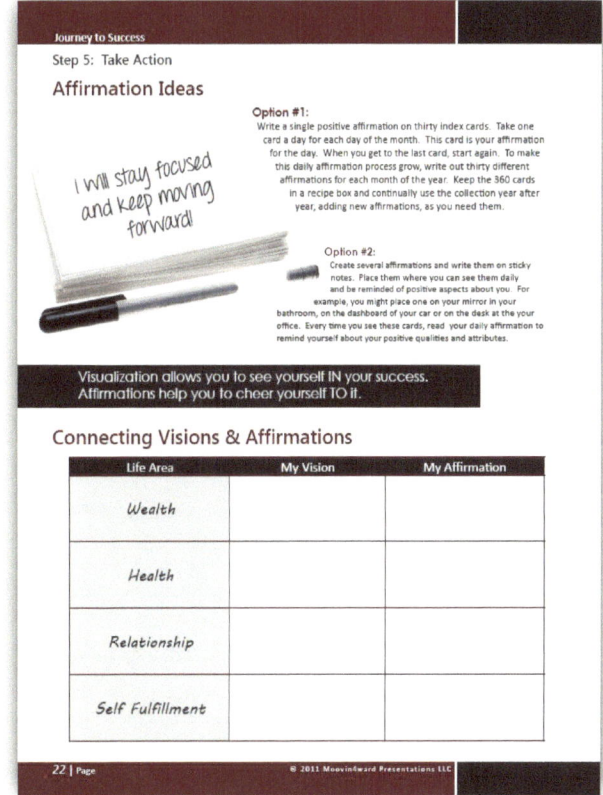

What's your perspective now on your _journey to success_? Do you expect the _journey to success_ will be lined with roses?

Why not? Will you throw in the towel and abandon your goals?

[Allow 1 minute for participants to respond to the questions.]

J2S Program Facilitator's Guide

Hard Work

[2 minutes]

Not everyone who's on top today got there with success after success. More often than not, those who history best remembers were faced with numerous obstacles that forced them to work harder and show more determination than others.

Yet, the world seems to be unwilling to admit that simple, good, old-fashioned hard work can be the basis of success.

Studies are constantly being made to determine personalities, hormone ratios, childhood characteristics, intelligence, education, methods, techniques, and the rationale of successful people. The fact that they work hard is shoved aside as some strange coincidence. **Take a look at page 23.**

Thomas Edison tried futility for years to convince the world that his inventions were not the result of any great genius he had. "Genius is one percent inspiration and 99 percent perspiration," was the way he explained it. "I never did anything worth doing by accident nor did any of my inventions come by accident; they came by work."

He left, at the time of his death, some 2500 notebooks crammed with notes of his work and ideas. He would work himself into virtual exhaustion and then sleep on a cot he had in his laboratory until sufficiently refreshed to pursue his work again.

It would be difficult to argue that **Michael Jordan** wasn't the greatest to ever step on a basketball court (yeah yeah, Kobe this, LeBron that). But Jordan wouldn't have been Jordan without a lot of hard work, dedication and yes, failure. Practicing hours before school and not resting until he had eliminated the weaknesses in his game.

"I've missed more than 9000 shots in my career. I've lost almost 300 games. 26 times, I've been trusted to take the game winning shot and missed. I've failed over and over and over again in my life. And that is why I succeed."

You heard it told that **Michael Jackson** "had a gift," "he was born with it," or "he was lucky." But if the truth is to be told, he worked his butt off. What people saw on stage at his peak was a culmination of decades of grueling hours of dedication to his work and perfecting his craft.

His childhood consisted of him spending thousands of hours in the studio rehearsing, practicing, and ensuring he hit every note. He carried that mindset into adulthood, spending several consecutive days and nights in the studio to fine-tune every second of his individual records.

Walt Disney was fired by a newspaper editor because "he lacked imagination and had no good ideas." But he had big dreams. After a number of his businesses ended in bankruptcy and failure, he eventually made his dreams come true with a lot of vision, planning, and hard work.

And the list goes on and on. Visit www.onlinecollege.org and search for "the 50 famously successful people who failed first." *[Add any other relevant "hard working" examples or ask participants for other names.]*

So the best kept secret of success seems to be that success, strangely enough, *is always preceded by hard work.*

Self-Motivation

[5 minutes]

Hard work and motivation go hand in hand. Motivation is one of the most important prerequisites for achieving one's goals. People who are successful at reaching their goals have done so because they have stayed motivated.

Staying motivated when things don't go the way you want can be difficult. But keeping a positive attitude can help you stay committed, motivated, and inspired.

Motivation is important to meet goals and finish projects. Some people may be very self-driven and others may need a high level of motivation to finish a task. It's very important that you know what motivates you personally.

Again, when you don't know what your purpose is, or you don't know where you want to go, it's hard to develop the motivation to go anywhere.

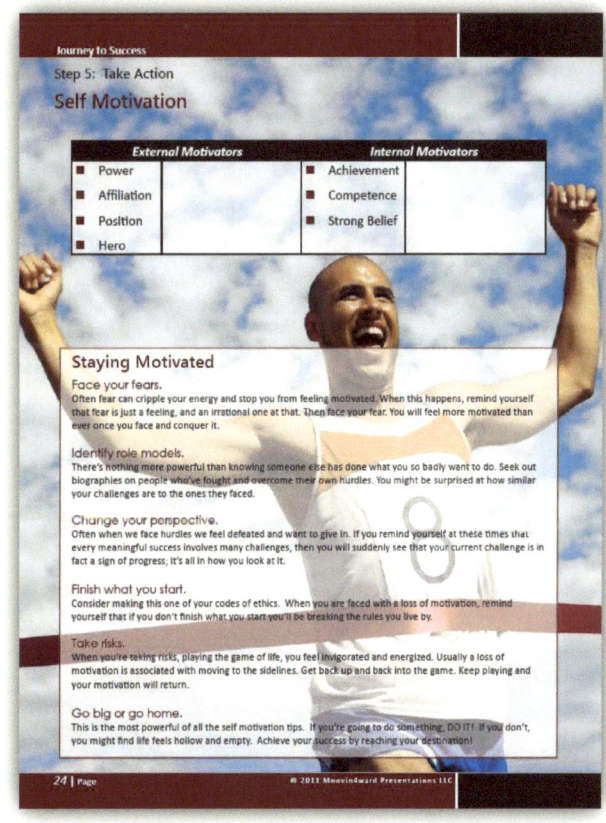

Most people who live without a purpose get tied up in the day-to-day monotony of life, like paying bills, cleaning and just getting by.

When you have a larger purpose, you elevate yourself above these concerns. Yes, they're still important and you still have to do them but your focus is on something much bigger. So first things first: make sure you are sure of what your purpose is before you look to motivate yourself.

Sources of Motivation

So it's important to examine what motivates you to move forward. Researchers have studied what motivates people and have identified two types of motivators: *internal* (inside a person) or *external* (outside a person). Most people aren't motivated by just one or the other, but some combination of the two.

Let's examine the two types of motivators. **Turn to page 24 in your workbook.**

External Motivators

When people are externally motivated, it's what they can get that motivates them to do or continue doing something. Externally motivated people are driven to act by things like money, material goods, being promoted, or receiving recognition.

Here are a few external motivations and examples:

- **Power:** The desire to seek control or have your opinions drive what others do is the motivation. *Example: To be the one who chooses which design to use for invitations to an annual event.*

- **Affiliation:** The desire to be with other people while accomplishing certain goals is the motivation. *Example: To work with the kids in the class who like science the most on a group science project.*

- **Position:** The desire to "move up the ladder" in a group to the top position is the motivation. *Example: To be shift manager at a part-time job.*

- **Hero:** The desire to do well in the eyes of someone you admire or respect, or to be like that person, is the motivation. *Example: To show your coach you can do your best time ever at the final season competition.*

Take a few moments to list three (3) external motivators for you, if any. *[Allow 1 minute. Ask volunteers to share.]*

Internal Motivators

When people are internally motivated, no amount of money, recognition, or other external item you offer, will be motivating. Internally motivated people are driven by how *they* feel about their *own* actions.

Here are a few internal motivations and examples:

- **Achievement**: The desire to achieve something, to work for the challenge rather than the reward, is the motivation. *Example: To participate in a 30-mile walk-a-thon.*

- **Competence:** The desire to master a job or do your best is the motivation. *Example: To learn how to use a software product.*

- **Belief in Something:** The desire to uphold personal values or ethics or fight for an individual belief is the motivation. *Example: To support animal rights.*

Take a few moments to list three (3) internal motivators for you, if any. *[Allow 1 minute. Ask volunteers to share.]*

How many of you are more externally motivated? *[Raise your hand to encourage responses.]* How many of you are more internally motivated? *[Encourage discussion.]*

Staying Motivated

It's an expected part of any journey of value that you'll lose motivation at some point. **Real journeys are transformational.** They change who you are as you pave your way. And a loss of motivation usually occurs right before a significant shift is set to take place.

Let me give you a few tips to help you stay motivated. You can write these in **your workbook on page 24.**

Face your fears. Often fear can cripple your energy and stop you feeling motivated. When this happens, remind yourself that fear is just a feeling, and an irrational one at that. Then face your fear. You will feel more motivated than ever once you face and conquer it.

Seek out role models. Read about people who've achieved what you want to achieve. There's nothing more powerful than knowing someone else has done what you so badly want to do. It lets you know that your goal is possible. Seek out biographies on people who've fought and overcome their own hurdles. You might be surprised at how similar your challenges are to the ones they faced.

Change your perspective. Often when we face hurdles we feel defeated and want to give in. If you remind yourself at these times that every meaningful success involves many challenges, then you will suddenly see that your current challenge is in fact a sign of progress; it's all in how you look at it.

Finish what you start. Consider making this one of your codes of ethics. When you are faced with a loss of motivation, remind yourself that if you don't finish what you start you'll be breaking one of the rules you live by.

Take risks. A loss of motivation can come when we feel paralyzed in having to do something outside of our comfort zone. When you're taking risks or daring yourself to do something out of the box, you feel invigorated and energized.

And finally, the most powerful of all the self motivation tips:

Always go big… or go home. If you're going do something, DO IT! If you don't you might find life feels hollow and empty. Achieve your success by reaching your destination!

> **We have learned that there are no shortcuts to success, except for hard work.**
> *To be successful in what you do you need to prioritize your work and take one task at a time. Believing in yourself and keeping yourself motivated and determined to achieve your goals will go a long way in helping you to enjoy success.*

As Abraham Maslow said:

> *"If you deliberately plan on being less than you are capable of being, then I warn you that you'll be unhappy for the rest of your life."*

When you're doing what you love or going after what you truly desire you'll struggle much less frequently with how to develop motivation. And the only time, if ever, that you'll need some outside help is when you're managing your resistance to change (i.e. your ego).

We've now covered the fifth step of the PSSP, let's review.

What was Step 1? *[Wait for participants to state, "Determine Your Destination."]*

What is Step 2? *[Wait for participants to state, "Identify Your Purpose."]*

What is Step 3? *[Wait for participants to state "Set Your Goals."]*

What is Step 4? *[Wait for participants to state "Develop Your Strategies."]*

What is Step 5? *[Wait for participants to state "Take Action."]*

Excellent!

Step #6: Evaluate Your Progress

Although you have determined your destination, identified your purpose, created great goals, visualized your success, and are ready to daily recite your affirmations, your PSSP is not complete until you have outlined your plan to evaluate your progress along your journey.

For example, have you ever gone on a trip to visit someone for the first time and were given landmarks?

Consider these landmarks as your milestones, your short-term goals that you must accomplish before you reach your final destination. Every landmark that you reach, is a goal achieved.

If you planned to reach one of these goals within a certain time frame *and you don't*, then you need to stop and determine where you are and how far you are away.

Did you miss a turn? Are you going in the right direction? Once you've identified how far you are off course, make the appropriate adjustments to get back on track.

Keep in mind that we are on a *journey*... to success. Even with a GPS to guide us on our way—our PSSP—there will always be some unforeseen encounters.

Some roads that you plan to travel will be under construction, so you'll need to expect detours, decreased speed limits, and roadblocks along the way. Take this opportunity to evaluate your progress. The process of reflection and evaluation allows us to ask, "Am I there yet?" and "Am I still on track and on schedule?"

How do you measure success? *[This is your lead in to the Measuring Success activity.]*

Activity 6.1: Measuring Success

Time: 10 minutes

Materials: Student Workbook page 25, three Agree/Disagree placards

Process:

So how do we measure success? I'll need three volunteers to come up front and help me with this. *[Select diverse volunteers.]*

The rest of you can follow along with us on page 25. Okay, I'll give each of you a card that reads "AGREE" on one side and "DISAGREE" on the other. I'll read the statement and you show the side of the card that fits your choice. Are we ready?

[After you read a question, allow a few seconds for participants to display their answer. Remember to engage the audience, but protect the participants if their answer varies from the majority.]

1. Success is measured by wealth, fame and power. Unless you have those three things, you are not successful.
2. Success is measured by happiness. If you are not happy in your life, then you are not successful.
3. Success can only be measured by your parents. If you fulfill the wishes and dreams of your parents, you are successful.
4. Since success is the opposite of failure, you are successful only when you don't fail.
5. Success can only be measured by achieved goals. If you have not achieved all of your goals, you are not successful.
6. Success cannot be measured because it is a continuous and ever-lasting process.

Just as the definition of the word success is different for everybody, so is the means to evaluate it. There is no best answer for this question. Similarly, there is no one way to measure or evaluate success.

Ultimately, success if personal. You define what it means to you and measure based on your definition.

[Thank your participants and instruct them to return to their seats. Consider giving each a participation gift.]

Progress Evaluation Process
[3 minutes]

There is no *one way* to measure or evaluate *success*. However, we **can** measure or evaluate our *progress* by tracking your completion of goals. **On the top of page 26** is the Progress Evaluation Process or PEP.

Let's walk through it together.

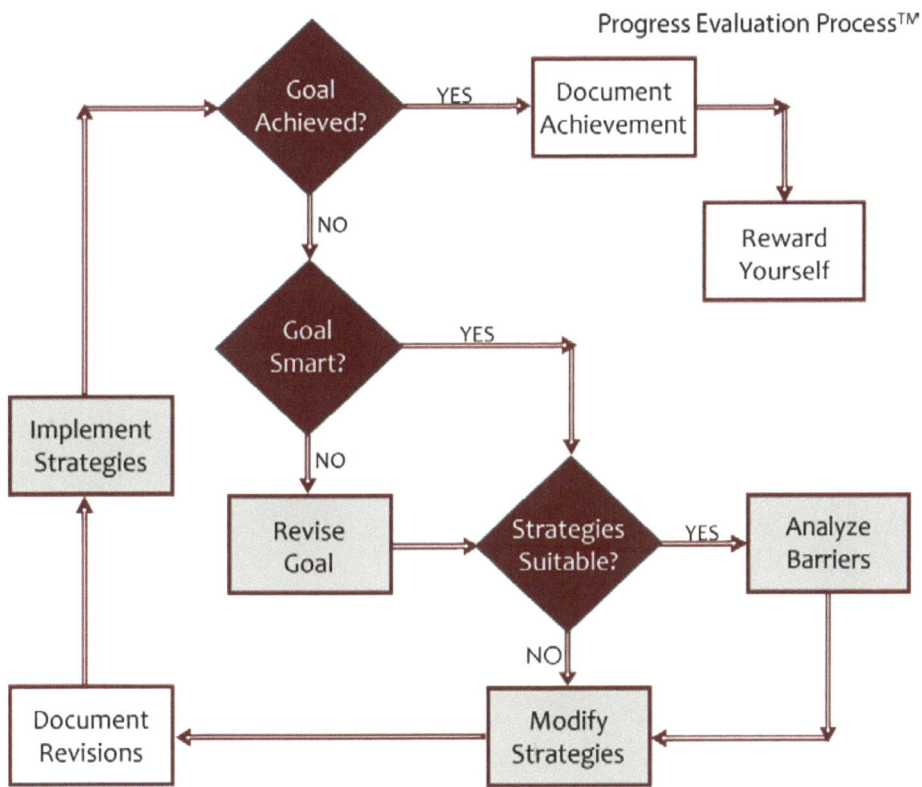

Let's start at "Goal Achieved". The first question is, *"Did you achieve your goal?"* If you did achieve your goal, **document** your achievement in your PSSP and then **reward yourself**.

If your goal was not achieved, we need to determine why. Ask yourself the second question, *"Was my goal a SMART goal?"* Review the goal to ensure that you accurately used the SMART framework that was discussed in Step 4. If the goal is not SMART, **revise the goal**.

If the goal was SMART and/or you revised the goal to ensure it was SMART, ask yourself the final question, *"Were my strategies suitable for the goal?"*

Review the strategies assigned to the goal and determine whether the strategies are all appropriate to help you accomplish the goal. If not, **modify the strategies**.

If the strategies are indeed fitting, then you'll need to **analyze the potential barriers** that may be hindering you from accomplishing the goals. We'll talk more about those in a moment. Once the barriers have been identified and removed, modify your strategies to accommodate your expected results.

The next action is to **document all revisions** to goals and strategies in your PSSP. Now it's time to once again **implement the strategies**.

Let's discuss the key actions involved in the PEP in more detail.

Review & Revise Goals

One of the reasons why you may not have achieved your goal is because you did not accurately use the SMART framework to establish that goal. So the first thing you'll want to do is ensure is that your goal is indeed specific, measurable, attainable, relevant and time-bound, as discussed in Step 3.

While you are reassessing your goals be mindful that you don't want to set goals that are harmful to you. For example, setting a goal to stop eating to lose weight can be destructive. You also want to be careful to not set goals that are contradicting to others, or to set wrong goals altogether.

If you find that your goals are indeed good goals, continue with the PEP to the next step. Otherwise, make the necessary revisions to your PSSP and start again.

Review, Revise & Implement Strategies

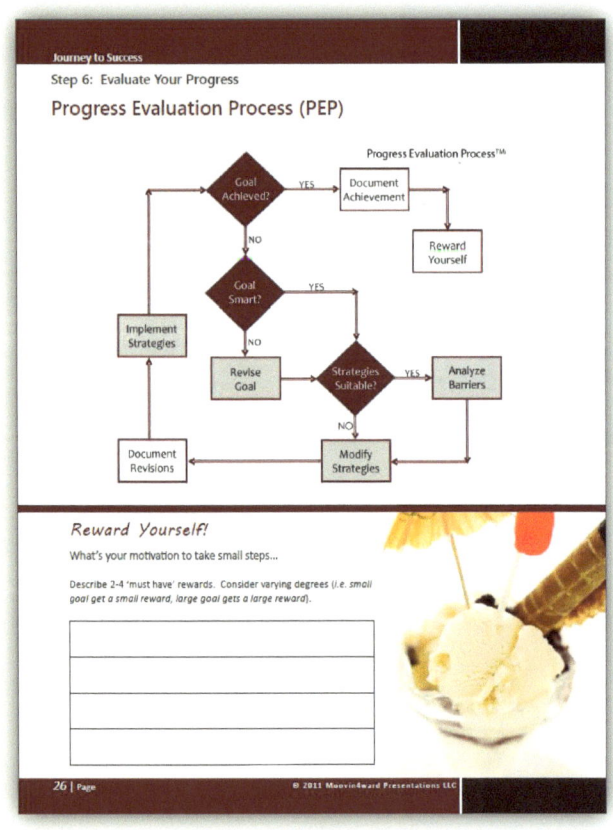

The next step is to review the strategies assigned to the goal and determine whether the strategies are all effective and productive to help you accomplish the goal. For example, let's say that your goal is to get a promotion at work. One of your strategies is to take the lead on several work projects. This is a fitting strategy. Unfortunately, with the additional tasks you are unable to accomplish any one project because you are overloaded. Being unproductive will likely not help you earn that promotion.

Again, if the strategies are not suitable, modify them. If the strategies are indeed fitting, then continue to the next step. Otherwise, make the necessary revisions to your PSSP and start again.

Reward Yourself

Let's talk about those rewards.

If you still wonder how to stay motivated, then note that rewarding yourself with every small success, with every small achievement, is very essential.

Most of us want and need to be rewarded for our achievements. With rewards, you can be motivated and start working with renewed inspiration and passion towards your success!

At the **bottom on page 26,** list 2-4 of your must have rewards. Select one for the quick and easy accomplishments and at least one for a major accomplishment. *[Allow one minute and then ask for volunteers to share.]*

Be sure to promise yourself a reasonable reward once you have achieved your goal. Let the idea of the tantalizing reward become your source of motivation. Your self-motivation will increase enormously if you give yourself a pat on the back for a job well done.

Your reward doesn't have to cost a lot. In fact, it doesn't have to cost anything, i.e. lounging and watching your favorite television show, working on your favorite hobby or enjoying some new music. Therefore, rewarding is one of the best self-motivation strategies.

Document Your Accomplishments

[2 minutes]

The entire PSSP process is all about helping you to document your plan for success. Your PSSP includes your destination, your purpose, your goals, and your strategies, along with any revisions or modifications. It will also include the actions you've taken, your accomplishments and your rewards.

*[Have a participant to read the second paragraph **on page 27,** or several participants to read a sentence of the second paragraph.]*

We all have our own stories of perseverance; how we've fought against defeat and found the strength to continue following our PSSP to achieve our goals. But when your journey is a lengthy one, you sometimes forget what you've accomplished. You forget how far you've come.

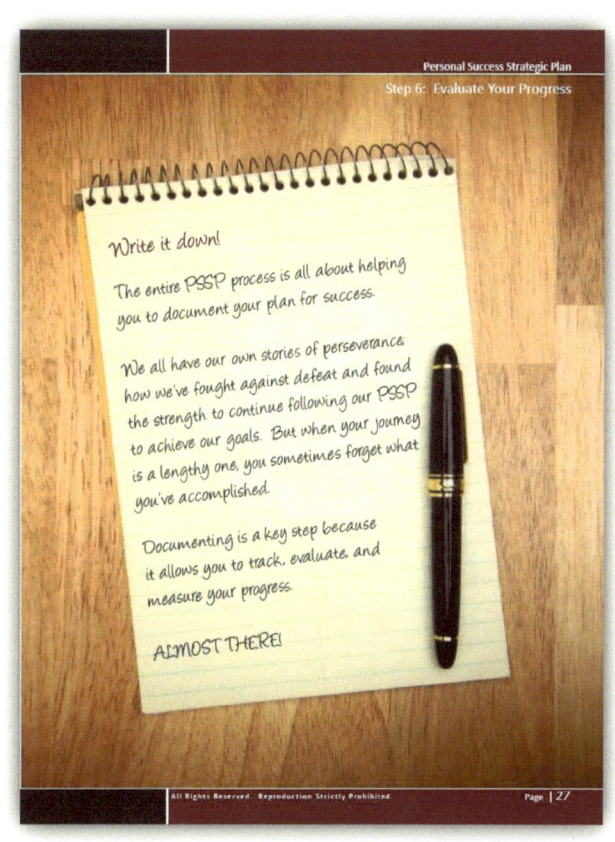

<u>Documenting is a key step because it allows you to track, evaluate, and measure your progress.</u>

Once upon a time, before computers and apps, a voyager would document his travels in a travelogue or road journal. Consider your PSSP as your travelogue. It is your historical progress report.

Analyze the Barriers

If you've set SMART goals and your strategies are suitable to help you achieve those goals, you need to analyze the barriers that may be blocking you from achieving your goals. **On page 28,** please write in these barriers as we review them.

[Be prepared to share some real examples or ask for examples from the participants.]

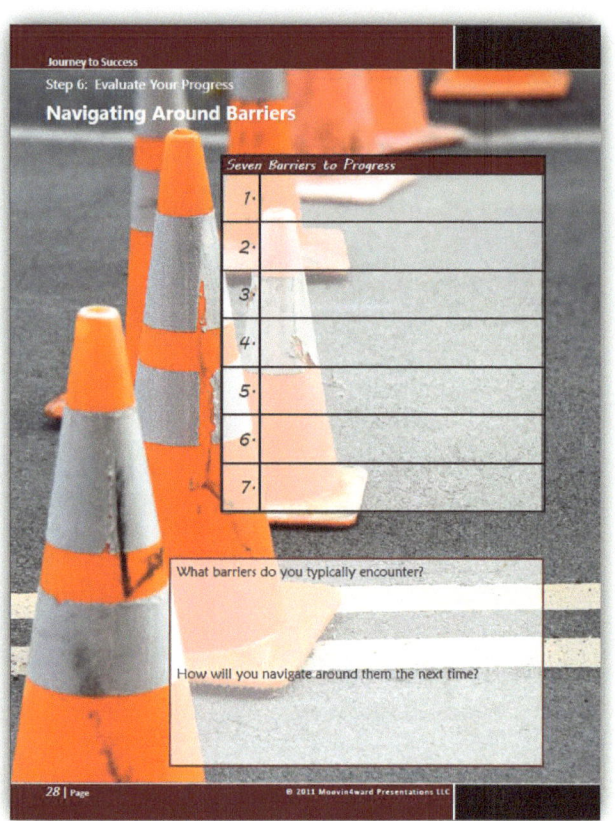

1. Navigating Frustration

Sometimes you work hard trying to achieve your goal and all goes well. But sometimes, when all doesn't go well, you experience frustration. The solution for dealing with this problem is to first, NOT beat yourself up. Second, you should divert your attention to how you can benefit from the setbacks.

Be sure to not set goals that highlight your weaknesses or you will create new frustrations and possibly additional setbacks.

2. Navigating Over Planning

Too much planning can be counter-productive. It is easy to do, but you need to realize what actually helps you achieve your goal is *taking action*. Action is acting upon your goals and NOT keeping yourself busy. Keeping busy on unproductive tasks, such as planning and redoing plans, is an utter waste of time. Focus on the most important things if you want to get results... **taking action** to your plans.

3. Navigating Too Much Talking

Talking about your plans can also be counter-productive. Announcing your plan to others satisfies your self-identity just enough that you're less motivated to do the hard work needed.

In 1933, W. Mahler found that if a person announced the solution to a problem, and was acknowledged by others, it was now in the brain as a "social reality," even if the solution hadn't actually been achieved.

In other words, once you've told people of your intentions, it gives you a "premature sense of completeness." Unless you are sharing your plans with someone that will help to hold you accountable, try to keep your plans private until you have accomplished your goals.

4. Navigating Fear

Some people are afraid they will fail, or even worse, they may actually succeed. As such, they don't even bother trying to attain goals. Such people lack belief in themselves and in their potential. In their mind, if they fail, everyone will think negatively of them. And if they succeed, people will be envious and think negatively of them. So it becomes a lose-lose situation no matter how they look at it. But realize that you can achieve anything you set your mind to. Believe in yourself and your abilities and others will too.

5. Navigating Overload

Again, the only time you fail is when you give up. If you have followed the goal setting steps outlined in Step 3, you will know that breaking up your difficult or complicated goals into small, easy, doable chunks is important. When you do this, your plan becomes a 'checklist'. What happens when you start completing these mini-tasks? You build momentum and eliminate feeling overloaded or overwhelmed.

6. Navigating Unsupportive People

Take a step back and assess the situation. Before you consider someone unsupportive, ensure that you have been clear in communicating your goal. If you haven't, try to be more descriptive and patient. If you have, depending upon the relationship, determine if you should take heed to their advice or ignore them totally. Sometimes your goals are just not in line with other people's goals; as a result they will try to pull you in another direction.

7. Navigating Loss of Commitment

One reason why people don't achieve their goals or reach their destination is because they lose their commitment. One great way to get your commitment level back up to par is to review your PSSP regularly. This will help to remind you why you are on the journey in the first place. Success comes when you are committed and driven to make it happen.

Those are some of the primary barriers to success. By show of hands *[raise your hand]*, how many of you battle with the first barrier of Frustration? *[Allow participants to respond.]*

How about Over Planning? *[Allow participants to respond. Continue through all of the barriers.]*

If any of these barriers are preventing you from reaching your goals, deal with them immediately and you'll soon be back on track to complete your journey.

Session 4: PSSP Review & Challenge
Workshop Script

Action Plan Format

Something magical happens when you develop a PSSP. Your desires go from being pie-in-the-sky daydreams to real and tangible possibilities. They then have the power to start guiding our actions and behaviors to bring them into reality.

When your goals are merely inside your head, managing any resistance to change is difficult if not impossible. But once they're on paper, you're on your way to turning dreams into reality.

This simple exercise of developing and documenting your roadmap for success greatly increases your chances of reaching the finish line. As you crystallize what tasks are required to achieve your dreams, you're programming your mind to prepare to take all the necessary steps that are required.

Now that we've covered all the tools needed, it is the time to produce your PSSP. All of the exercises we've completed provide you with a jumpstart.

Let's review the Six Steps to PSSP **on page 29 in your workbook**.

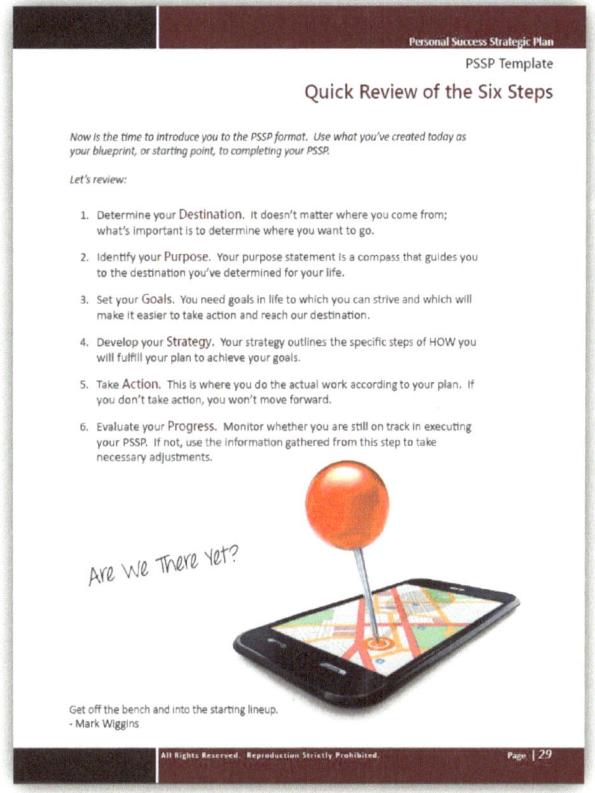

1. Determine Your **Destination**.
2. Identify Your **Purpose**.
3. Set Your **Goals**.
4. Develop Your **Strategy**.
5. Take **Action**.
6. Evaluate Your **Progress**.

Turn to your PSSP template in your workbook which starts **on page 30**. Using all of the data from your notes, I'm going to allow you the next 20 minutes to build a draft of your PSSP. I recommend reviewing your plan over the next few days to fine tune it. You'll only be completing the first four sections. The rest you'll complete throughout your journey.

> **Remember that your PSSP is a living and breathing document.**
> *This means that as life happens, changes may occur. You may even get sidetracked and not progress as you thought you would. But when it happens, it's OK. If you review your PSSP often and are willing to make adjustments along the way, you will stay on course to reach your destination.*

[Allow participants 20 minutes to complete the template and ask any questions.]

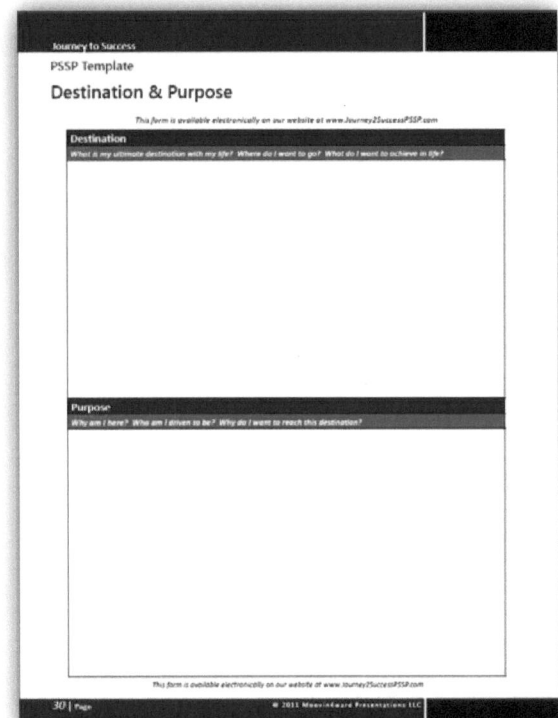
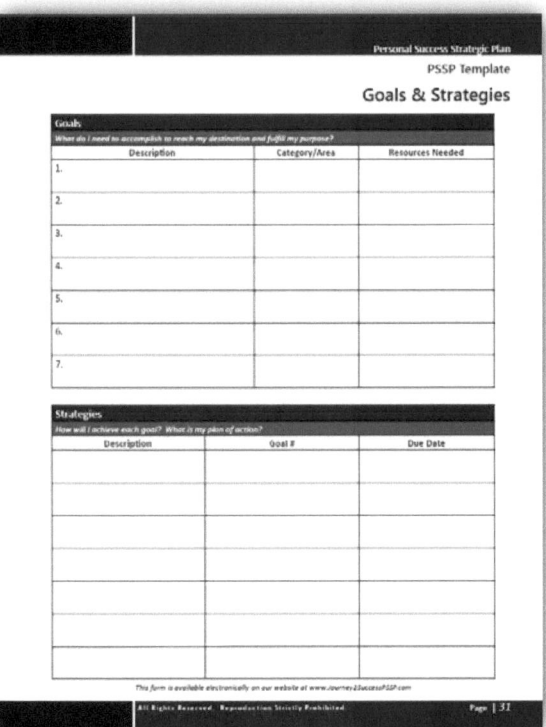
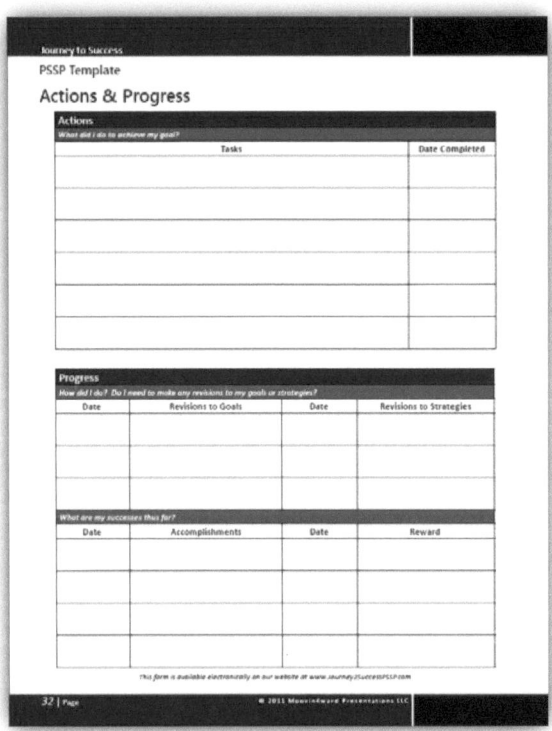

Personal Success Strategic Plan (PSSP)

The PSSP Challenge

Let's have some fun to see what you've learned.

Activity 7.1: **PSSP Pyramid Game**

Time: 30 minutes

Materials Projector, PSSP Pyramid Slides (which can be downloaded from the J2S website), 2 chairs, stopwatch, paper

Process:

[Be sure the set up the room prior to starting the game. Your pyramid game should be displayed on the projector. One player has their back to the screen, the other faces the screen. Select someone to keep the time and another to keep the score. Before you begin, be sure to review the rules and objectives.]

We're going to play the game Pyramid. We're going to need several teams of two to compete.

[You'll need at least two teams (pairs) to have a competition. There are a total of six rounds plus a lightening round.]

The objective of the game is to name as many of the elements in a selected category as possible within 2 minutes. Each category will have only 7 elements.

One of you will be able to see the answers and will have to describe the answers to your partner without using the actual answer. Your partner will have to guess the answer based strictly on your clues. You can choose to pass to save time, if necessary. You cannot use the element in the description or you lose that element.

Which team is ready? *[After a team has come forward, ask them to decide who will give and who will receive.*

Choose a category.

[Read the participants the first slide of the category, which is a description of what will need to be described. Tell the time-keeper to get ready by putting 2 minutes on the timer. When participants are ready, click to the next slide which will show the first element. Repeat until game is done.

The team that wins the most points or the most categories may participate in the Lightening Round. The team will have 1 minute to name all of the categories in this final round.]

J2S Program Facilitator's Guide

In Closing

Remember that no one becomes successful by accident. Success requires making a plan and sticking to it. By following the simple steps we've outlined in this program, you can become successful and achieve all that you hunger for.

It's simple, but requires commitment; it's not hard to do, but requires hard work. The good news is that once you begin, the results will start coming almost instantly.

The miracle of successful living is that the smallest step towards success attracts more success! Everybody experiences fear of failure, uncertainty, insecurity, low self-esteem, indecision, depression, nervousness and embarrassment.

Successful people master these temporary conditions by taking positive action, by sticking to their plan, by maintaining their vision of the future, by learning from setbacks and by rededicating themselves to the pursuit of their purpose.

By following the six steps we've outlined to develop your personal success strategic plan, you will not only reach your destination, you'll grow from and through the journey.

Success is Personal!

Success is Moovin4ward!

One-Hour Script
Plenary Session

A Journey to Barcelona

[2 minutes]

Let's go on a journey.

What is a journey? *[Wait for a few answers.]*

One definition states that a journey is an occasion when you travel from one place to another, especially when there is a long distance between the places.

Based on this definition, you need to know where YOU ARE and then the place YOU WANT TO GO.

So let's say we want to go to Barcelona, Spain. Every summer they host a huge carnival with an abundance of feasting, dancing, and partying in the streets. I've always dreamed of going there during that time. You would expect that this would be a journey of a lifetime, something you'll never forget. So you'll want to do more than a weekend visit.

So first, we'll go on the Internet to see how far away it is. Wow. That's a true journey. Is this really where we want to go? Yes! We only live once!

So what do we need to do to make this happen? *[Poll the participants for a list of things that may need to be done to make the journey happen. Expect responses such as: get a passport, find lodging, book a flight, learn the weather, buy new clothes, learn Spanish, etc.]*

It won't happen overnight. We'll need to make lots of arrangements and save some money. The goal is to get there within the next five years. We'll need a minimum of $10,000 in cash, because we don't want to do it on credit. We want to come home from our journey debt free and smiling.

So we will need to pay off all of our current debt then start to save the money for the trip. We'll need to get a passport. We'll need to find a place to stay that won't require us to need transportation right away, except for the taxi from the airport. We'll need to find out what the weather is like, so we'll know how to pack. We'll need to learn some Spanish, because we want to be able to communicate.

There's a lot to do. Once we get our plan together, we can get started: saving money, learning Spanish, looking for housing, making our dream come true.

Now along the way, things may come up. I might lose my job, I might lose a loved one, I might encounter a medical emergency or natural disaster that depletes my savings… things, obstacles, unexpected challenges, might come along.

But when you are committed, it means that no matter what happens, you are going to fulfill your goal. Why? Because we have planned for it and want it badly, that's why. We may have to shift our schedule, stay at a lesser expensive hotel, or make other adjustments to the plan; but we are going to follow through with it.

 **Success is not one major event, but a series of achieved goals, that motivates you to keep moving forward.**

It all starts with creating your own *Personal Success Strategic Plan (PSSP)* and taking action according to your plan to reach *your* defined success. It requires a great bit of self-discipline, because it's a self-determined destination.

Open your worksheet to the first page on the left. as I share the Six Steps to developing your PSSP.

Six Steps to PSSP

[1 minute]

1. Determine Your **Destination**. It doesn't matter where you come from; the most important key is to determine where you want to go.

2. Identify Your **Purpose**. It is your compass that guides you and drives you to what you want to do with your life.

3. Set Your **Goals.** You need to have personal goals in life to which you can strive and which will make it easier to reach your destination.

4. Develop Your **Strategy.** Your strategies are the steps you plan to take in order to make your goals a reality.

5. Take **Action.** This is where you make it all happen; do what you've planned.

6. Evaluate Your **Progress**. Check yourself periodically to ensure you stay on track and make adjustments as needed.

"The journey of a thousand miles starts from a single step." Your first step on your journey to success starts with your PSSP. Through the program, I will guide you to develop your own PSSP.

Personal Success Strategic Plan (PSSP)

Step #1: Determine Your Destination

Let's play a game. I'll need three volunteers to assist me. *[Select three diverse volunteers.]*

> **Activity P1:** **Donkey Tail**
>
> **Time:** 7 minutes
>
> **Materials:** Donkey poster, three donkey tails in a box hidden in the audience, 1 blindfold, 1 map, and 1 plan (list of specific instructions to find the hidden donkey tails).
>
> We're going to play an old game, "Pin the Tail on the Donkey?" We're going to see which of your peers can pin the tail on the donkey first. *[Point to the donkey poster on the easel.]*
>
> Now, what is your name? Okay, Name 1, you get to be blindfolded. *[Tie blindfold on the first volunteer.]* What's your name? Okay, Name 2, you get this. *[Hand the second volunteer the map.]* And now what's your name? Okay, Name 3, you get this *[Hand student the instructions.]*
>
> Okay, you guys have 5 minutes to pin the tail on the donkey. Go! *[Don't give any additional instructions. Just let it play out. Once the third volunteer has pinned the tail on the donkey, call "TIME."]*
>
> So how was that? Let's start with Name1. Why didn't you pin the tail on the donkey? *[Allow discussion with the volunteer and the audience. We are looking for "couldn't see the donkey and/or it moved."]*
>
> How about you, Name 2. Why didn't you pin the tail on the donkey? You could see it and you had a map. *[Allow for discussion with the volunteer and the audience (i.e. "the map didn't help" or "it didn't give any information".]*
>
> And lastly, Name 3. Why was it so easy for you to pin the tail on the donkey? *[We are looking for "I could see where I needed to go," or "I had instructions."* So you had a plan that was specific to your goal?
>
> How helpful would it be to have a step-by-step plan for a successful life?

To be successful in life, it's important to define what success means to you personally. Your destination is your success. Once you've determined your destination, you can create step-by-step instructions to reach it.

Journey to Success Program

True Meaning of Success

[3 minutes]

We all have goals we'd love to achieve, but the sad truth is that most of us will never achieve them. There have been plenty of studies done that show you how to achieve any goal. These studies illuminate what separates successful people from everyone else. But some people literally wander through life like player 2 and player 3 in our activity.

So what separates high achievers from everyone else? *[Allow a few moments for responses.]*

 **What separates high achievers from everyone else isn't ability or resources. It's hunger.**

Les Brown tells us, *"Wanting something is not enough. You must hunger for it. Your motivation must be absolutely compelling in order to overcome the obstacles that will invariably come your way.'*

Take a look at the bullets in the grey box on **page 2 of your worksheet.**

High Achievers are HUNGRY!

These individuals have a hunger to succeed is so great that it fuels them to follow through and to keep fighting no matter what circumstances they face.

They don't get discouraged when their faith is tested. They know that doubt is a virus of the mind.

They absolutely never entertain it. Instead, they quickly disregard it whenever it pays them a visit.

They are resilient enough to persist and keep on following through despite what their fears might tell them.

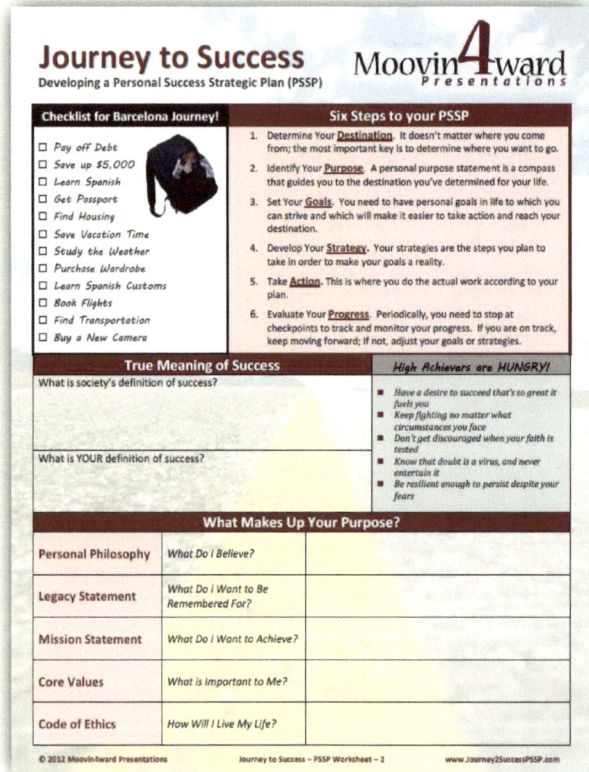

So how do you reach a state of hunger for success? *[Allow a few moments for thought.]*

First we must define success. What is the TRUE meaning of success?

Let's answer these questions together **on page 2** under "True Meaning of Success."

[Ask the following questions and allow time for responses]

- What is the social definition of success?

- How do you personally define success? What will success look like for you 20 years from now?

How does *your* definition of success differ from *society's* definition of success? *[Ask for volunteers to share their differences.]*

Keep in mind that it is perfectly fine that your definition matches or doesn't match society's definition. The point here is that it's YOUR definition that you're trying to attain.

 **A personal success strategic plan is critical if you want to achieve your personally defined true meaning of success**.

Why? Because achieving goals requires transformation on a mental and physical level, and a plan helps with managing resistance to change, which naturally arises when you make any significant shifts in your life.

People often begin setting goals without a solid destination of what they ultimately want to achieve. But if you don't have a destination in mind, then you'll never know which road to take to get where you want to go. Your destination needs to be clear—something you can visualize and describe to others. Without a clear view of what you want in life, you'll be forever changing course and falling short of your potential.

Now we've covered the first step of the PSSP, which is… *[Allow participants to state "Determine your Destination."]*

Let's move to Step 2.

Journey to Success Program

Step #2: Identify Your Purpose

It All Starts with You
[6 minutes]

In life, we think we know where we want to go… our success. But when our success doesn't match our purpose, we tend to encounter numerous roadblocks and don't quite understand why.

Imagine you want to become an architect because your family has always told you that you were a great artist, a prerequisite for becoming an architect. So they say.
After years of college, you determine that your purpose in life is to help motivate children through art. While your destination was associated with art, becoming an architect was not your purpose in life.

 **You can significantly increase the odds of success in any endeavor, if you know who you are, what you want, where you are going, how you will get there, and what you will do once you arrive.**

Follow along in your worksheet at the **bottom of page 2** as we seek to understand the "questions" that provide us with the "answers" that summarize WHO YOU ARE. Let's start with your personal philosophy.

1. Personal Philosophy

Every person has a personal philosophy, consisting of some rules adopted from one's parents, culture, religion, environment, and so on.

- Not consuming meats and becoming a vegetarian
- When and how you worship, if at all
- Not to smoke cigarettes
- How you care for pets
- Using products made of animals
- Using only recycled materials

Generally speaking, these rules are not always well thought out and contain a wealth of inconsistencies and contradictions.

Your personal philosophy answers the question, "What do I believe?"

On your worksheet, write one of your personal philosophies. *[Allow 1 minute.]*

Personal Success Strategic Plan (PSSP)

2. Legacy Statement

Your legacy serves as your life's defining statement. It provides an overarching framework for all mission statements and goals to follow.

Let's try this, I'll name a person and you tell me what their legacy in one word. *[Read one at a time and allow time for responses to each. Be sure to consider your audience when you select a name to choose appropriate persons.]*

- Mahatma Gandhi – *[peace, non-violence]*
- Martin Luther King – *[equality, civil rights, non-violence]*
- Steve Jobs – *[innovation, technology]*
- Michael Jackson – *[pop music, dance]*
- Princess Diana – *[charity]*

Okay, what legacy would you say the following *will* leave behind? *[Read one at a time and allow time for responses to each.]*

- Bill & Melinda Gates
- Oprah Winfrey
- Lebron James

Your legacy statement answers the question, "What do I want to be remembered for?"

On your worksheet, write the one word that would describe the legacy you will leave behind. *[Allow 1 minute.]*

3. Mission Statement

A mission statement is a declaration of who you are, why you exist, and what you intend to accomplish. You can't exactly choose what legacy you leave behind, but you can choose what you want to achieve in your life that will contribute to the legacy you leave behind.

- Al Gore: *"… my goal is to share with you both my passion for the Earth and my deep sense of concerned for its fate."*
- Oprah Winfrey: *"To help women see every experience and challenge is an opportunity to grow and discover their best self."*

Your mission statement answers the question, "What do I want to achieve?"

4. Code of Ethics

Ethics are a personal code of behavior. For the most part they will help define what you do with your life, the career you choose, whether you have a family, whether you marry, and/or how you'll treat others.

That's because who you are defines your ethics and your ethics define who you are. It is a joined circle. Codes of conduct, personal creeds, and pledges all reflect an effort to make sense of things, to organize behavior, and to better understand ourselves.

Your future and the future of our world depend on how you behave.
Examples of personal codes of ethics:
- "I will maintain my physical and emotional health through regular exercise, good eating habits, and the proper care of my body."
- "I will continue to grow intellectually through personal study, comprehensive reading, and attending growth conferences."
- "I will be honest and responsible in my finances by paying all debts on time and not living a lifestyle above my means."

Your code of ethics answers the question, "How will I live my life?"

5. Core Values

Our values act as our compass, guiding us through life's terrain. Values represent an individual's highest priorities and deeply held driving forces that motivate our actions. In other words, we make choices based on our values. **Look at the list of values on the right column of page 3.**

Examples of values:

Ambition	Courage	Honesty	Accomplishment
Competency	Wisdom	Teamwork	Credibility
Individuality	Independence	Excellence	Privacy
Equality	Security	Accountability	Recognition
Integrity	Challenge	Empowerment	Appreciation
Service	Influence	Quality	Reputation
Responsibility	Learning	Efficiency	Democracy
Accuracy	Compassion	Dignity	Purity
Respect	Friendliness	Collaboration	Stability
Dedication	Discipline/Order	Stewardship	Wealth
Diversity	Generosity	Empathy	Dependability
Improvement	Persistence	Pleasure	Power/ Authority
Enjoyment	Optimism	Change/Variety	Knowledge

So how do you know which are most important to you? We can all glance at this list and feel as though most are equally important. So let's do a quick exercise to help.

Personal Success Strategic Plan (PSSP)

> **Activity P2:   My Values**
>
> **Time:** 3 minutes
>
> **Materials:** Participant worksheet, page 3, right column
>
> Put a square around your 15 must have values. This won't be easy, but make your best effort. *[Allow about 60 seconds. Begin calling out a few of the values and providing examples. Some participants will need to understand the values in context.]*
>
> Now of those 15 in squares, put a star by the 8 that are very important to your well-being. *[Allow another 60 seconds. Participants will begin to grumbling about the difficulty of the task. Motivate them through it.]*
>
> Of those 8 with stars, which four would you give up? Cross those out. *[Allow 30 seconds.]*
>
> Of the four remaining, circle the two that you could not live without. These are the ones that drive your actions.

Your core values answer the question, "What is important to me?"

Back on **page 2 on your worksheet**, list your top two core values. *[Allow 30 seconds.]*
Your answers to all of these questions provide fuel for achievement, and are the reasons behind all of your actions and inactions.

Successful people know what they want, how and when they will achieve it, but most importantly they know WHY they want to become successful at achieving their goals.

Step #3: Set Your Goals

[5 minutes]

As the cliché goes, if you don't know where you're going, how will you ever know if you arrived? In addition to knowing your purpose in life, you also need to set goals to help you get where you want to go in life.

A **_Goal_** is something that someone wants to achieve and is an important fundamental element to developing a sound PSSP.

Why is goal setting important anyway? How else can you hope to achieve your true meaning of success? Goal setting helps you to develop motivation and forces you to focus your time and energy.

When you lack goals, it's difficult to avoid just drifting through life as your day-to-day decisions have no larger purpose. Hence the saying, "If you aren't sure where you're going, any road will lead you there."

Set SMART Goals

Now that you know why having goals is important, you need to understand that not just any goal will do. We want to be sure that we set SMART goals.

SMART is an acronym that stands for all of the qualities and characteristics your goals should have in order to increase your likelihood of success.

SMART is a system or a framework for judging the components of your goal. It stands for:

S	Specific
M	Measurable
A	Attainable
R	Relevant
T	Time-bound

Let's review each of these attributes. **Please take notes on the top of page 3.**

Specific

Do you know exactly what you want to accomplish?

To achieve a goal, you need to be specific about what it is. Otherwise it's difficult to turn your vision into set tasks. To be specific, your goal should state clearly what you intend to accomplish. This will allow you to know exactly what you're working toward.

- *Bad example: "I want to become healthier."*
- *Good example: "I want to become healthier by changing my diet to replace junk food with fruits and increase my workouts to three times a week."*

Measurable

Are you able to assess your progress?

Making a goal measurable makes it possible to monitor your progress. It also forces you to become clear on where you're starting from, which is always important. If your goal is too undefined, you'll find it's impossible to tell when you have even achieved it. Your goal is measurable if you are 100% clear what success will look like and what failure will look like.

- *Bad example: "I want to be rich."*
- *Good example: "I want to generate a quarter of a million dollars in liquid income within 10 years from today."*

Attainable

Is your goal within your reach given your current situation?

Research has shown that one of the most important elements of success is having a goal that's achievable. It's easy to get caught up wanting to do something HUGE. But the problem is: it's difficult to stay motivated over the long run if your goal seems unattainable. You will easily feel hopeless and abandon your efforts.

To ensure your goal will motivate you, break a really large goal down into smaller ones. At the same time, you don't want your goal to seem too small. The best size is one that stretches you without breaking you.

- *Bad example: "I want to become a millionaire in 2 months."*
- *Good example: "I want to become a millionaire within 10 years by starting my own business and winning government contracts to provide services in warzone countries."*

Relevant

Is your goal pertinent towards your destination and purpose in life?
A goal is relevant if it elevates you to your larger goals, your overall purpose. Remember that your goals are intended to help you reach your ultimate destination, and therefore should not divert you from that achievement.

Let's say that your long term goal is to purchase a home and it will take you five years to save the down payment. But in the short-term, you decide to take a two-week vacation in Las Vegas with friends, which will use up two years of your savings. It seems that your short-term goal is in conflict with your bigger vision.

- *Bad example: "After I earn my degree in agriculture, I want to become a rap star."*
- *Good example: "Before I graduate with my degree in agriculture, I want to work an internship with a large company in the agriculture industry."*

Time Bound

What is the deadline for completing your goal?

Deadlines are critical. They keep you in action and they keep you motivated. Without a time limit there's no urgency to start taking action now.

Make sure you are realistic with your time frame. There's nothing less motivating than missing your goal all because you didn't allow yourself the right amount of time.

- *Bad example: "I am going to work on my project."*
- *Good example: "I am going to finish my project by Sunday evening at 8pm and I'll achieve this by working six hours on Saturday evening and six hours on Sunday afternoon."*

Make sure that you follow the SMART framework when developing your goals and you'll increase your likelihood of success.

Goal setting allows us to be proactive, instead of just being reactive. Goal setting is just the first step to achievement.

Step #4: Develop Your Strategy

[6 minutes]

Remember that goals need a plan of action.

Imagine, for instance, that your goal is to get an internship position. Knowing that your goal has to be SMART, you list that you want to get an internship position for a company based in Washington, DC by the summer of your junior year. Sounds SMART.

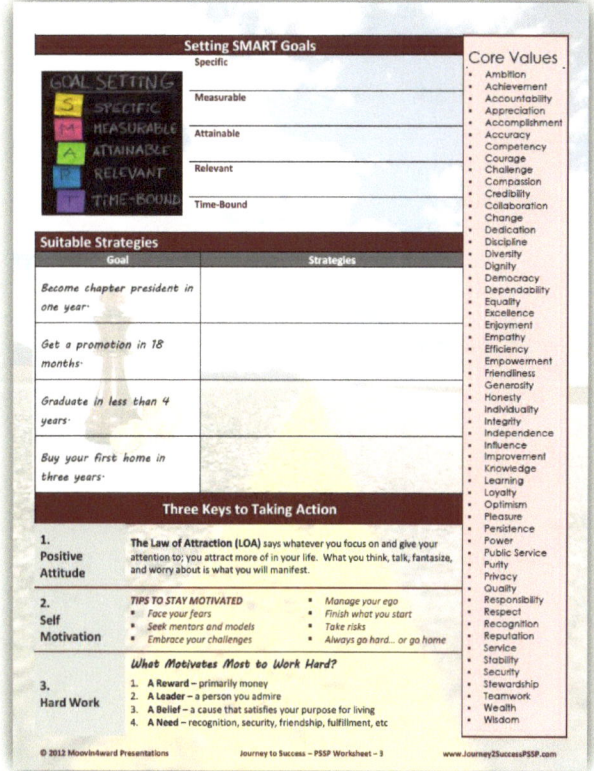

Time passes. May of your junior year rolls around and you don't have an internship position. While you started out well, by setting a SMART goal to achieve, *you didn't perform any action to help you achieve the goal*.

What's missing from this scenario is a strategy to help you accomplish the goal you have set. You didn't register with the career development office; that's a strategy. You didn't search for or submit any applications; those are strategies.

Not having a strategy is like trying to pin the tail on a donkey when you're blindfolded. You don't have a chance.

 **Your strategy is simply your plan of action that you will execute to accomplish your goals.**

What will you do to make success a reality based on the goals you've set?

Developing Strategies

[5 minutes]

In selecting your strategies, make sure they are suitable for the goal you are trying to accomplish. Your intent is to develop a plan of action that will allow you to actually achieve your goal.

If your strategies are not appropriate and suitable for the goals you are trying to achieve, then YOU'LL FAIL! For example, if your goal is to lose 25 pounds and your strategy is to stop eating, you will more than likely fail or starve to death trying.

Let's say you have a SMART goal to lose 25 pounds in six months. What strategies or plan of action might you take to achieve your goal? *[Encourage participants to respond. We are looking for "change your diet, exercise regularly, fasting", etc.]*

Excellent. Let's try another one.

Look at the middle of page 3 on your worksheet. Here we have several goals listed. Let's walk thru them.

Let's say you have just joined a new student organization on campus and your goal is to become chapter president by the next year. What strategies might you take to achieve your goal? *[We are looking for "actively participate, review the requirements in the bylaws, start campaigning, track your contributions", etc.]*

Great!

One more: if you wanted to earn a degree in less than four years, skipping classes and/or interning would not be suitable strategies for your goal. What strategies might you take to achieve your goal? *[We are looking for "taking extra courses, go to school during the summer months, etc."]*

Good job!

Step # 5: Take Action

[7 minutes]

Now it's time to get moving; time to take action and make it happen. There are three key components needed to get you going. You must have a **positive attitude**, be **self-motivated**, and **work hard**. You need to have and maintain these qualities in order to persevere to your final destination.

Positive Attitude

If you are serious about creating a successful life for yourself, you need to start by cultivating the right attitude.

Whether or not you have a positive attitude right now, you can adopt one. Remember, a positive attitude isn't a feeling. It's a state of mind. You develop a positive attitude by *deciding* you'll respond positively to life circumstances, no matter what.

There will be days when it's difficult to maintain a positive attitude, but don't be discouraged. What separates high achievers from everybody else is their ability to regain their positive attitude after they have fallen off the wagon. Be sure you get right back on again.

Most importantly, resolve to start right now to be more positive. Always look for *how* you can do something rather than *why* you can't. Believe in yourself no matter what. And be disciplined enough to continuously seek ways to improve. If you do this diligently, in time you will start to experience the truly life-changing benefits of a positive attitude.

Law of Attraction

The Law of Attraction (LOA) says that whatever you focus on and give your attention to; you attract more of in your life. What you think, talk, fantasize, and worry about is what you'll manifest.

The most important part of the law of attraction is that you always need to think positive and believe in your goals without having any doubts in your mind.

Creative visualization and affirmation in achieving goals are the two most popular techniques used by many people and recommended by the masters of LOA.

Visualization Techniques

The first step of visualization is to find your goal and make an action plan to achieve it. You must take a few minutes of your day to imagine that you have achieved your goal.

Try to take a mental picture of the day of your success and hold on to the feelings that you will feel the moment you will reach your goal. Most importantly try to interact with the day of your success in your mind.

Try to feel what it's like to have your friends congratulate you on your success.

Understanding Affirmations

Affirmations are a useful tool to help change the beliefs, images and thought processes that you have within you. It is a "self-talk" that affirms you positively or negatively.

For example, how often have you said to yourself "No, I'm not good at...?" or "Yes, I can do this!" These are both affirmations, but affirmations that can either prevent you from moving forward to accomplishment or propel you.
Take a look at the top of page 4.

There are three statements that shape positive self-talk
- **I AM** – a statement of who you are.
- **I CAN** – a statement of your potential.
- **I WILL** – a statement of positive change in your life.

I AM statements are positive affirmations of a real state of being that exists in you.
- ☑ I am competent.
- ☑ I am patient.
- ☑ I am forgiving.

I CAN statements are positive affirmations of your ability to accomplish goals.
- ☑ I can lose weight.
- ☑ I can let go of guilt.
- ☑ I can handle my course load.

I WILL statements are positive affirmations of a change you want to achieve.
- ☑ I will like myself better each day.
- ☑ I will graduate with honors.
- ☑ I will let go of past mistakes.

Affirmations are a way of starting and ending each day. By learning to consciously verbalize positive thoughts to ourselves, we will reap the benefits of positive thinking.

Positive affirmation are a fundamental part of using the Law of Attraction, and anything that helps you to keep remembering and repeating your affirmation, you must use.

 **Use of positive affirmations and visualizations on a regular and consistent basis will support your success.**

Hard Work

Not everyone who's on top today got there with success after success. More often than not, those who history best remembers were faced with numerous obstacles that forced them to work harder and show more determination than others.

Yet, the world seems to be unwilling to admit that simple, good, old-fashioned hard work can be the basis of success.

Studies are constantly being made to determine personalities, hormone ratios, childhood characteristics, intelligence, education, methods, techniques, and the rationale of successful people. The fact that they work hard is shoved aside as some strange coincidence. **Take a look at page 23.**

Thomas Edison tried futility for years to convince the world that his inventions were not the result of any great genius he had. "Genius is one percent inspiration and 99 percent perspiration," was the way he explained it. "I never did anything worth doing by accident nor did any of my inventions come by accident; they came by work."

He left, at the time of his death, some 2500 notebooks crammed with notes of his work and ideas. He would work himself into virtual exhaustion and then sleep on a cot he had in his laboratory until sufficiently refreshed to pursue his work again.

It would be difficult to argue that **Michael Jordan** wasn't the greatest to ever step on a basketball court (yeah yeah, Kobe this, LeBron that). But Jordan wouldn't have been Jordan without a lot of hard work, dedication and yes, failure. Practicing hours before school and not resting until he had eliminated the weaknesses in his game.

"I've missed more than 9000 shots in my career. I've lost almost 300 games. 26 times, I've been trusted to take the game winning shot and missed. I've failed over and over and over again in my life. And that is why I succeed."

You heard it told that **Michael Jackson** "had a gift," "he was born with it," or "he was lucky." But if the truth is to be told, he worked his butt off. What people saw on stage at his peak was a culmination of decades of grueling hours of dedication to his work and perfecting his craft.

His childhood consisted of him spending thousands of hours in the studio rehearsing, practicing, and ensuring he hit every note. He carried that mindset into adulthood, spending several consecutive days and nights in the studio to fine-tune every second of his individual records.

Walt Disney was fired by a newspaper editor because "he lacked imagination and had no good ideas." But he had big dreams. After a number of his businesses ended in bankruptcy and failure, he eventually made his dreams come true with a lot of vision, planning, and hard work.

And the list goes on and on. Visit www.onlinecollege.org and search for "the 50 famously successful people who failed first." *[Add any other relevant "hard working" examples or ask participants for other names.]*

So the best kept secret of success seems to be that success, strangely enough, *is* always preceded by hard work.

Self-Motivation

Hard work and motivation go hand in hand. Motivation is one of the most important prerequisites for achieving one's goals. People who are successful at reaching their goals have done so because they have stayed motivated.

Staying Motivated

It's an expected part of any journey of value that you'll lose motivation at some point. **Real journeys are transformational.** They change who you are as you pave your way. And a loss of motivation usually occurs right before a significant shift is set to take place.

Let me give you a few tips to help you stay motivated. You can follow along on **your worksheet on the bottom of page 3.**

Face your fears. Often fear can cripple your energy and stop you feeling motivated. When this happens, remind yourself that fear is just a feeling, and an irrational one at that. Then face your fear. You will feel more motivated than ever once you face and conquer it.

Seek out mentors and role models. Read about people who've achieved what you want to achieve. There's nothing more powerful than knowing someone else has done what you so badly want to do. It lets you know that your goal is possible. Seek out biographies on people who've fought and overcome their own hurdles. You might be surprised at how similar your challenges are to the ones they faced.

Change your perspective. Often when we face hurdles we feel defeated and want to give in. If you remind yourself at these times that every meaningful success involves many challenges, then you will suddenly see that your current challenge is in fact a sign of progress; it's all in how you look at it.

Finish what you start. Consider making this one of your codes of ethics. When you are faced with a loss of motivation, remind yourself that if you don't finish what you start you'll be breaking one of the rules you live by.

Take risks. A loss of motivation can come when we feel paralyzed in having to do something outside of our comfort zone. When you're taking risks or daring yourself to do something out of the box, you feel invigorated and energized.

And finally, the most powerful of all the self motivation tips:

Always go big… or go home. If you're going do something, DO IT! If you don't you might find life feels hollow and empty. Achieve your success by reaching your destination!

As Abraham Maslow said:

> *"If you deliberately plan on being less than you are capable of being, then I warn you that you'll be unhappy for the rest of your life."*

When you're doing what you love or going after what you truly desire you'll struggle much less frequently with how to develop motivation. And the only time, if ever, that you'll need some outside help is when you're managing your resistance to change (i.e. your ego).

Step #6: Evaluate Your Progress

Have you ever gone on a trip to visit someone for the first time and were given landmarks to guide you?

Consider these landmarks as your milestones, your short-term goals that you must accomplish before you reach your final destination. Every landmark that you reach, is a goal achieved.

If you planned to reach one of these goals within a certain time frame *and you don't*, then you need to stop and determine where you are and how far you are away.

Or maybe you ask, "Did you miss a turn?" "Are you going in the right direction?" Once you've identified how far you are off course, make the appropriate adjustments to get back on track.

Keep in mind that we are on a *journey*... to success. Even with a GPS to guide us on our way—our PSSP—there will always be some unforeseen encounters.

Some roads that you plan to travel will be under construction, so you'll need to expect detours, decreased speed limits, and roadblocks along the way. Take this opportunity to evaluate your progress. The process of reflection and evaluation allows us to ask, "Am I there yet?" and "Am I still on track and on schedule?"

How do you measure success? *[This is your lead in to the Measuring Success activity.]*

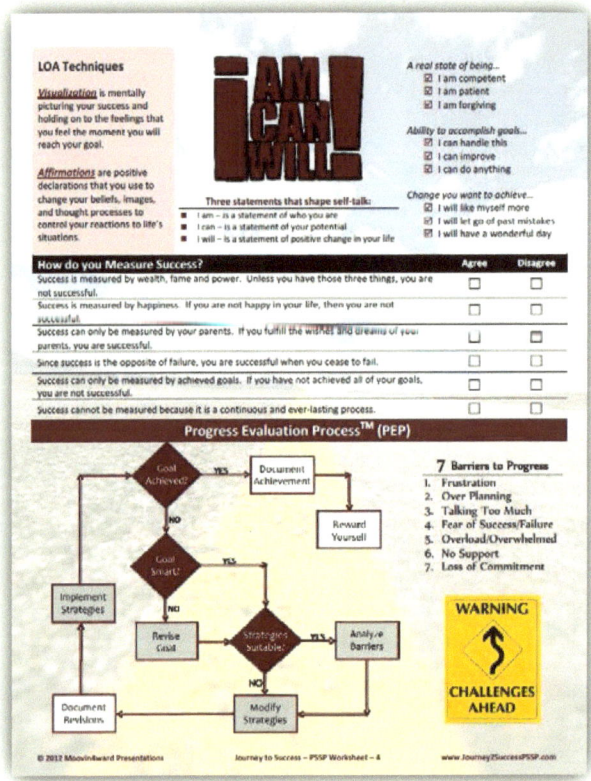

Personal Success Strategic Plan (PSSP)

Activity P3: Measuring Success

Time: 10 minutes

Materials: Participant Worksheet, page 4, three Agree/Disagree placards

So how do we measure success? I'll need three volunteers to come up front and help me with this. *[Select diverse volunteers.]*

The rest of you can follow along with us on the center of page 4. Okay, I'll give each of you a card that reads "AGREE" on one side and "DISAGREE" on the other. I'll read the statement and you show the side of the card that fits your choice. Are we ready?

[After you read a question, allow a few seconds for participants to display their answer. Remember to engage the audience, but protect the participants if their answer varies from the majority.]

1. Success is measured by wealth, fame and power. Unless you have those three things, you are not successful.
2. Success is measured by happiness. If you are not happy in your life, then you are not successful.
3. Success can only be measured by your parents. If you fulfill the wishes and dreams of your parents, you are successful.
4. Since success is the opposite of failure, you are successful only when you don't fail.
5. Success can only be measured by achieved goals. If you have not achieved all of your goals, you are not successful.
6. Success cannot be measured because it is a continuous and ever-lasting process.

Just as the definition of the word success is different for everybody, so is the means to evaluate it. There is no best answer for this question. Similarly, there is no one way to measure or evaluate success.

Ultimately, success if personal. You define what it means to you and measure based on your definition.

[Thank your participants and instruct them to return to their seats. Consider giving each a participation gift.]

Progress Evaluation Process

[4 minutes]

There is no *one way* to measure or evaluate *success*. However, we **can** measure or evaluate our *progress* by tracking your completion of goals. **On the bottom on page 4** is the Progress Evaluation Process or PEP.

Let's walk through it together.

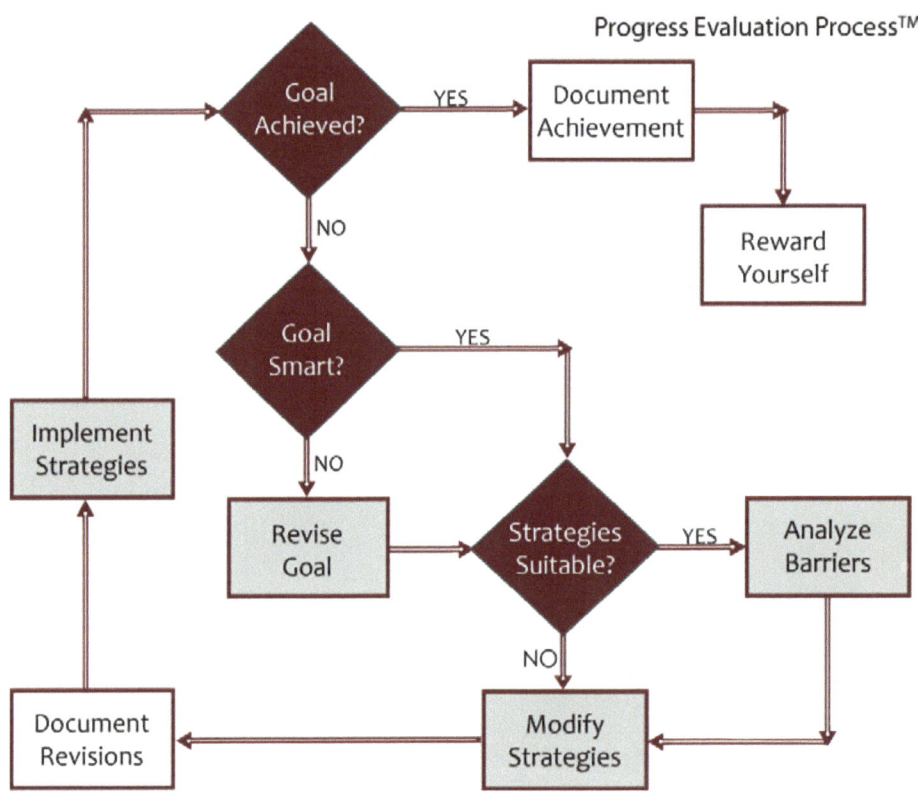

Let's start at "Goal Achieved". The first question is, *"Did you achieve your goal?"* If you did achieve your goal, **document** your achievement in your PSSP and then **reward yourself**.

If your goal was not achieved, we need to determine why. Ask yourself the second question *"Was my goal a SMART goal?"* Review the goal to ensure that you accurately used the SMART framework that was discussed in Step 4. If the goal is not SMART, **revise the goal**.

If the goal was SMART and/or you revised the goal to ensure it was SMART, ask yourself the final question, *"Were my strategies suitable for the goal?"*

Review the strategies assigned to the goal and determine whether the strategies are all appropriate to help you accomplish the goal. If not, **modify the strategies**.

If the strategies are indeed fitting, then you'll need to **analyze the potential barriers** that may be hindering you from accomplishing the goals. We'll talk more about those in a moment. Once the barriers have been identified and removed, modify your strategies to accommodate your expected results.

The next action is to **document all revisions** to goals and strategies in your PSSP. Now it's time to once again **implement the strategies**.

Let's discuss the key actions involved in the PEP in more detail.

Review & Revise Goals

One of the reasons why you may not have achieved your goal is because you did not accurately use the SMART framework to establish that goal. So the first thing you'll want to do is ensure is that your goal is indeed specific, measurable, attainable, relevant and time-bound, as discussed.

While you are reassessing your goals be mindful that you don't want to set goals that are harmful to you. For example, setting a goal to stop eating to lose weight can be destructive. You also want to be careful to not set goals that are contradicting to others, or to set wrong goals altogether.

If you find that your goals are indeed good goals, continue with the PEP to the next step. Otherwise, make the necessary revisions to your PSSP and start again.

Review, Revise & Implement Strategies

The next step is to review the strategies assigned to the goal and determine whether the strategies are all effective and productive to help you accomplish the goal. For example, let's say that your goal is to get a promotion at work. One of your strategies is to take the lead on several work projects. This is a fitting strategy. Unfortunately, with the additional tasks you are unable to accomplish any one project because you are overloaded. Being unproductive will likely not help you earn that promotion.

Again, if the strategies are not suitable, modify them. If the strategies are indeed fitting, then continue to the next step. Otherwise, make the necessary revisions to your PSSP and start again.

Reward Yourself

Let's talk about those rewards.

If you still wonder how to stay motivated, then note that rewarding yourself with every small success, with every small achievement, is very essential.

Most of us want and need to be rewarded for our achievements. With rewards, you can be motivated and start working with renewed inspiration and passion towards your success!

Be sure to promise yourself a reasonable reward once you have achieved your goal. Let the idea of the tantalizing reward become your source of motivation. Your self-motivation will increase enormously if you give yourself a pat on the back for a job well done.

Document Your Accomplishments

The entire PSSP process is all about helping you to document your plan for success. Your PSSP includes your destination, your purpose, your goals, and your strategies, along with any revisions or modifications. It will also include the actions you've taken, your accomplishments and your rewards.

We all have our own stories of perseverance; how we've fought against defeat and found the strength to continue following our PSSP to achieve our goals. But when your journey is a lengthy one, you sometimes forget what you've accomplished. You forget how far you've come.

Documenting is a key step because it allows you to track, evaluate, and measure your progress.

Analyze the Barriers

If you've set SMART goals and your strategies are suitable to help you achieve those goals, you need to analyze the barriers that may be blocking you from achieving your goals. **On page 28, please write in these barriers as we review them.**

1. Navigating Frustration

Sometimes you work hard trying to achieve your goal and all goes well. But sometimes, when all doesn't go well, you experience frustration. The solution for dealing with this problem is to first, NOT beat yourself up. Second, you should divert your attention to how you can benefit from the setbacks.

Be sure to not set goals that highlight your weaknesses or you will create new frustrations and possibly additional setbacks.

2. Navigating Over Planning

Too much planning can be counter-productive. It is easy to do, but you need to realize what actually helps you achieve your goal is *taking action*. Action is acting upon your goals and NOT keeping yourself busy. Keeping busy on unproductive tasks, such as planning and redoing plans, is an utter waste of time. Focus on the most important things if you want to get results... **taking action** to your plans.

3. Navigating Too Much Talking

Talking about your plans can also be counter-productive. Announcing your plan to others satisfies your self-identity just enough that you're less motivated to do the hard work needed.
In 1933, W. Mahler found that if a person announced the solution to a problem, and was acknowledged by others, it was now in the brain as a "social reality," even if the solution hadn't actually been achieved.

In other words, once you've told people of your intentions, it gives you a "premature sense of completeness." Unless you are sharing your plans with someone that will help to hold you accountable, try to keep your plans private until you have accomplished your goals.

4. Navigating Fear

Some people are afraid they will fail, or even worse, they may actually succeed. As such, they don't even bother trying to attain goals. Such people lack belief in themselves and in their potential. In their mind, if they fail, everyone will think negatively of them. And if they succeed, people will be envious and think negatively of them. So it becomes a "lose lose" situation no matter how they look at it. But realize that you can achieve anything you set your mind to. Believe in yourself and your abilities and others will too.

5. Navigating Overload

Again, the only time you fail is when you give up. If you have followed the goal setting steps outlined in Step 3, you will know that breaking up your difficult or complicated goals into small, easy, doable chunks is important. When you do this, your plan becomes a 'checklist'. What happens when you start completing these mini-tasks? You build momentum and eliminate feeling overloaded or overwhelmed.

6. Navigating Unsupportive People

Take a step back and assess the situation. Before you consider someone unsupportive, ensure that you have been clear in communicating your goal. If you haven't, try to be more descriptive and patient. If you have, depending upon the relationship, determine if you should take heed to their advice or ignore them totally. Sometimes your goals are just not in line with other people's goals; as a result they will try to pull you in another direction.

7. Navigating Loss of Commitment

One reason why people don't achieve their goals or reach their destination is because they lose their commitment. One great way to get your commitment level back up to par is to review your PSSP regularly. This will help to remind you why you are on the journey in the first place. Success comes when you are committed and driven to make it happen.

Those are some of the primary barriers to success. By show of hands, how many of you battle with the first barrier of Frustration? *[Allow participants to respond. Continue through all of the barriers.]*

If any of these barriers are preventing you from reaching your goals, deal with them immediately and you'll soon be back on track to complete your journey.

Review & Summary

Something magical happens when you develop a PSSP. Your desires go from being pie-in-the-sky daydreams to real and tangible possibilities. They then have the power to start guiding our actions and behaviors to bring them into reality.

When your goals are merely inside your head, managing any resistance to change is difficult if not impossible. But once they're on paper, you're on your way to turning dreams into reality.

This simple exercise of developing and documenting your roadmap for success greatly increases your chances of reaching the finish line. As you crystallize what tasks are required to achieve your dreams, you're programming your mind to prepare to take all the necessary steps that are required.

Let's review the Six Steps to PSSP **on page 29 in your workbook**.

1. Determine Your **Destination**.
2. Identify Your **Purpose**.
3. Set Your **Goals**.
4. Develop Your **Strategy**.
5. Take **Action**.
6. Evaluate Your **Progress**.

Remember that no one becomes successful by accident. Success requires making a plan and sticking to it. By following the simple steps we've outlined in this program, you can become successful and achieve all that you hunger for.

It's simple, but requires commitment; it's not hard to do, but requires hard work. The good news is that once you begin, the results will start coming almost instantly.

By following the six steps we've outlined to develop your personal success strategic plan, you will not only reach your destination, you'll grow from and through the journey.

Success is Personal!

Success is Moovin4ward!

Personal Success Strategic Plan (PSSP)
Template

PSSP Template

Destination
What is my ultimate destination with my life? Where do I want to go? What do I want to achieve in life?

Purpose Statement
Why am I here? Who am I driven to be? Why do I want to reach my destination?

Goals
What do I need to accomplish to reach my destination and fulfill my purpose?

	Description	Category/Area	Resources Needed
1.			
2.			
3.			
4.			
5.			

Strategies
How will I achieve each goal? What is my plan of action?

Description	Goal #	Due Date

Actions
What did I do to achieve my goal?

Tasks	Date Completed

Personal Success Strategic Plan (PSSP)

Progress

How did I do? Do I need to make any revisions to my goals or strategies?

Date	Revisions to Goals	Date	Revisions to Strategies

What are my successes thus far?

Date	Accomplishments	Date	Reward

Notes

Become a Certified J2S Program Facilitator!

Visit www.Journey2SuccessPSSP.com/affiliation_program for training schedule or email affiliate@moovin4ward.com

SHARE WITH YOUR PARTICIPANTS

Test Your J2S Knowledge and earn a free J2S T-shirt

Simply pass the online quiz and post a photo of your score on the Moovin4ward Presentations Facebook page.

http://www.journey2successPSSP.com/PSSP_Quiz/PSSP_Concepts_Quiz.pdf

Purchase Workbooks

To order copies of the accompanying workbook at bulk pricing, contact

>Moovin4ward Presentations
>1-888-893-6303
>orders@moovin4ward.com
>www.journey2successPSSP.com